CHASING

NANCY DAILEY

This book is registered with the Library of Congress:
Library of Congress Control Number: 2017908571
A & S Publishing, Springfield, MO

Cover art and drawings by Nancy Dailey

Paperback-Press
an imprint of A & S Publishing
A & S Holmes, Inc.

ISBN: 1-945669-22-5
ISBN-13: 978-1-945669-22-4

DEDICATION

To Cara Dailey who started it all with the comment, "There's a lady you need to write a book about."

ACKNOWLEDGMENTS

My gratitude and thanks go to the many people who helped in any way to bring this book to fruition. It would be impossible to name everyone, but my thanks are no less sincere.

I have a deep appreciation for our interlibrary loan system which enabled me to research books in German that I would otherwise never have seen.

Thank you to the people in the archives and museums in Germany and Holland who so graciously answered my email enquiries, with special thanks to Jeltsje Boersma, a Guide of the Mummie Grafkelder at the church of Wiuwert for the very helpful packet.

Anke Wegner Ballhausen welcomed me into her home, and helped with transportation while I was in Frankfurt; thank you. And thank you Öznur Takil for taking time out from your own studies to bring me much appreciated additional information.

I am very grateful to the people who helped make my trip to Suriname possible: Bob and Diana Criger, Clarice and Larry Loehr, Miwa Muroga, Walt Waschick, Kay Gallagher, Beverly Crandell, Wanda Sue Parrott, Rose Lombardo, Rue and Tom Withers, Karen Falconer, and Naomi Shaw. My apologies if I have missed anyone.

I appreciate all the helpful notes and suggestions provided by critique group members and other readers.

My appreciation also goes to Brenna Waddell who took care of Darlun, Frankie, and my house while I was away.

To each and every one of you, as well as the people along the way who encouraged me to continue—Thank you.

NOTE FROM THE AUTHOR

In this biography I have created dialogue to bring Maria's story to life. There is no way to know what conversations took place; there were no magazine or newspaper articles about her, no personal diary. My efforts, though, have been to be as faithful as possible to her character based on the known facts.

There is no birth record for Maria. However, the custom in the 1600s was to baptize babies two days after birth. Her baptism record is dated April 4, 1647, so the assumption and accepted birthdate is April 2.

Maria's father, Matthäus Merian (the Elder), had grown children from a previous marriage. After his first wife died he married a younger woman, Johanna Heim, and together they had two children: Maria Sybilla and Maximillian. Apparently only one half-brother, Caspar, stayed in contact with Maria and her mother.

The spelling of names has not always been consistent. Even Maria sometimes spelled her middle name Sybilla instead of the more usual Sibylla. I have chosen to use the more unusual spelling to honor this unusual lady.

A long time ago...
before you could buy pans of watercolor paint in a
plastic case...
before there were tubes to hold paint...
before you could buy paint already made...
before there was even watercolor paper to paint
on...

    an artist was born.
        Her name was
            Maria Sybilla Merian

A long time ago...
before people understood that butterflies were not
witches...
before people knew that caterpillars were not the
work of the devil...
before people knew how to properly observe and
make notes of what they saw...
before there was even a word for it...

    a scientist was born.
        Her name was
            Maria Sybilla Merian

A long time ago...
before there were computers, packaged inks and printers...
before there were typewriters and inked ribbons...
before you could buy paper at a store...
before pencils, even...

a writer was born.
Her name was
Maria Sybilla Merian

A long time ago...
before women could get jobs outside the home...
before women could be members of a scientific group...
before women could attend universities...
before women could attend high school, even...

Maria Sybilla Merian
became the leading scientific authority on metamorphosis and the mother of entomology.

This is her story.

CHAPTER 1

Three year old Maria Merian reached for a caterpillar.

"Gott im Himmel, Maria Sybilla, don't touch that Devil's worm!" Her mother pulled her back. "Stay away from it."

Devil's worm? A caterpillar? Yes. In 1650 in Frankfurt, Germany, where the Merians lived, most people really believed that. Maria's mother did.

Maria's family consisted of herself, her mother Johanna, her father Matthäus, and her younger brother, Maximillian (or Max). Her father was elderly, and not well. In fact, he was sick when he married Johanna. Because of this Maria probably often heard her mama say, "Be quiet, Maria, little Max is sleeping." Or, "Be quiet, Maria, your papa is resting."

But Maria didn't want to be quiet. She probably

wanted to touch one of those worms the Devil had made.

In June her father made a decision. "It's time to make another trip to Langenschwalbach," he said. His pale face almost matched the white pillow of his bed.

"Are you up to such a journey?" asked Maria's mama.

"The hot springs helped so much last time. I'm sure they will again."

Maria looked at her parents. They sounded so serious. And what were hot springs?

The day to leave arrived.

Maria scrambled up the steps and into the coach. The four horses whinnied and stamped their feet. The carriage tilted slightly as her mother, carrying baby Max, and her father climbed in and settled on the cushions. When the driver closed the door, Maria looked out the window and watched him unhook the steps and store them in a rack behind the coach. Then he stepped out of sight.

The carriage dipped and rocked. Maria's eyes opened wide as she looked frantically around.

"It's all right, Liebchen," said her mother as she reached over and patted her daughter's arm. "The driver is putting our bags up on top of the carriage."

Finally, the driver sat down on the high seat in front, picked up the reins, and gave them a flick. The horses leaned forward and pulled.

The coach lurched as the wheels began moving. They were on their way.

Papa leaned back and closed his eyes. He winced

with every bump but didn't say anything. Her mother soothed little Max. Maria scooted as close to the window as she could get, eagerly watching everything.

When they turned north away from the Main River valley, the horses struggled to pull the heavy coach up the mountain. Maria had to hang on to stay in her seat. Her father moaned now and then.

Maria discovered Langenschwalbach was a place with warm water springs called a spa. Sick people believed the water would make them well.

Each time Matthäus was in the spa, his family went for a walk. It was no different on the evening of June nineteenth. Maria, her mother, and her little brother went for an evening walk around town. Her mother spoke with people she had met who had also come to the famous healing waters hoping for a cure.

Johanna Merian and her two children arrived back at the public house where they were staying and stepped inside. A group of people stood in the lobby. They turned, looking at her mother.

Mama's eyebrows rose, then drew together. She held Max closer and pulled Maria to her.

Maria didn't understand the word "died." Why was her mother sobbing? She grabbed her mother's skirt and buried her face in it.

CHAPTER 2

"No, you can't take over the business," declared a man Maria didn't know. He spoke loud; he frowned and clenched his jaw. Maria grabbed her mother's long skirt and hid behind it. She peeked out at the other people standing with him.

"You haven't even been here to help run the family business," her mother said. "It was my husband's business, now it's mine."

"You may be our stepmother, but you don't know anything about running a publishing company!" he shouted, He shook his finger at her.

"I—"

The angry man kept talking as she tried to speak. "This was my father's business, and it needs someone with a lot more experience than you have. It has been neglected during my father's illness. The business needs to be rebuilt by someone with

4

contacts all over Europe, contacts you do not have."

All of his brothers and sisters, her mother's stepchildren, agreed. "Matthäus and Caspar will keep the business. But we will give you some of the money. That's all." They handed Maria's mother a bag of coins. And left.

Her mother looked at the small bag in her hand. "That's all?"

During the following months Maria often saw her mother smooth and re-smooth the folds of her skirt. Sometimes she saw her mother sit at the table and empty the coins out of the bag. Her mother moved the coins around, putting them into stacks. There were less coins than there used to be. Her mother did not smile.

"I want you to make a good impression today, Maria."

Maria's mother glanced at little Max sitting in the small, dark brown padded leather chair. He waved a toy, sometimes hitting the wooden tray across the chair's arms in front of him.

There was a knock at the door. There stood a man with long, curly, brown hair.

"Hello, Jacob," said her mother. She smiled and stood aside to let him in.

Jacob Marell bent down level with the two children. The ends of his small brown moustache turned up when he smiled.

"Guten Tag, Maria. Guten Tag, Maximillian. What a big name for such a little boy."

Max banged his toy on the tray.

That was the first of many visits from Jacob

Marell.

Spring turned into the warmer days of summer. The few small, puffy clouds in the pale blue sky seemed to just hang overhead. Maria had to walk right up to the flowers in the garden before she could smell them now. When it was windy, the smells traveled to her.

Jacob and her mother talked about marriage. Jacob had become a citizen of Utrecht in the Netherlands when he lived there. Now he wanted to be a citizen of Frankfurt again before they married. (Citizenship back then was given by cities, not by countries.)

On Saturday, July 22, 1651, Jacob Marell came again. The ends of his moustache turned up as he smiled. "I am a citizen!" he said.

Two weeks later Jacob became Maria's stepfather. Since he had three children of his own Maria now had another sister and two more brothers. Sara was eight and Franciscus was seven; both were older than Maria. But Fredericus was three, only a little older than Max.

Maria, her mother and little Max moved in with Jacob and his children. Their belongings were sent to the Marell house. They walked with Jacob to their new house. Jacob opened the door. Maria hung back.

"Come, Liebchen, said her mother, giving a quick tug, "This is our home, now."

Maria touched the doorframe. What will it be like here? Will Sara and Franciscus like me? Will I like them? She slowly stepped inside. She looked around, then focused on the girl and three boys across the room. Three boys?

Jacob introduced his apprentice, Abraham Mignon.

"What's an apprentice?" asked Maria.

"An apprentice studies with a master artist," said Sara, "because he wants to become an artist, too. Abraham lives with us and learns from our papa." Sara stood tall with her chin held high. She looked directly at her father. "Papa is a master artist," she said.

Every morning the following week Maria watched as Sara, Franciscus, and Abraham left for school.

"I'd like to go to school," Maria sighed. Instead, she had to help her mother care for the two younger children. This was harder than just watching Max. Fredericus had a lot more energy, and he ran from one room to another. He liked to pull open the doors of cabinets and take things out. Max tried to keep up with him, but Max did not have the energy to run or to open doors. Mostly he just watched. After a while he no longer even tried to follow.

In late November little Maximillian Merian died. He was only two and a half years old.

"Is Max coming back?" asked Fredericus.

Maria watched as tears slid silently down her mother's face.

"No, Fredericus, Max is not coming back," said her mother.

"Like my papa did not come back," said Maria.

"Ja, Liebchen, just like your papa did not come back."

Maria frowned. She lowered her head, then stared sideways at Sara. She still has two brothers. I don't have any, now.

CHAPTER 3

Two years later, when the new school year began, Maria was up early. "Now I can go to school!" she chanted. She danced around the room. She sat down, she stood up. She looked from Sara and Franciscus to Abraham. "When do we leave?" she asked.

"After breakfast," replied Sara.

"I'm not hungry."

"We don't have to be there until 6:30," said Sara. "And I am hungry."

Every day for two years Maria, Sara, Franciscus, and Abraham left for school together. Then one day, as Maria reached for her book bag, she noticed that while Franciscus and Abraham were ready to go, Sara was not.

"Sara? Are you coming?"

"No, I cannot. I am too old for school, now. I am ten years old."

"Too old?" Maria looked puzzled. "But Franciscus is older than you, and he still goes to school."

"Well, he's a boy, and boys have to learn Latin."

"I want to learn Latin, too."

"Only boys learn Latin, silly. Girls don't need to know it."

"Why not?"

Sara rolled her eyes. "Because girls grow up, get married, and run a household. We don't need to know Latin for that."

Maria crossed her arms and frowned.

When they came home from school one day to eat lunch, her mother told Maria to set the table. She told Sara to tell those in the studio the food was ready.

Maria looked up when Sara returned with her father and Abraham. Another, older boy walked into the room with them. Maria paused with a plate half way to the table.

"This is Johann Andreas Graff," said Jacob. "He is also apprenticing with me."

"Will he go to school with us?" asked Maria.

Both Jacob and Johann shook their heads.

"I am finished with school," said Johann. "I will spend all my time now learning more about art."

"Are there any girls who are apprentices?" asked Maria.

Johann smirked,

"No," said her stepfather.

"Why not?"

"Being an apprentice is part of the studies needed for a man to become a master artist. Girls don't become master artists."

Maria's mouth turned down. Something else girls can't do.

Later Maria slipped into her stepfather's studio. Jacob was not there, but the two apprentices were. She walked over to see what Johann was painting.

"Don't come over here, little girl." He stuck out his hand, fingers spread, towards her.

She stopped, her eyes wide.

"I don't want you to mess up my work," he said.

"She won't do that," said Abraham from across the room. "She just watches, and maybe asks a few questions. She won't touch anything."

Johann said nothing; He looked at her and scowled. Maria scowled back.

Abraham motioned Maria over to him. He stopped grinding with the mortar and pestle as she approached,

"What color pigment are you making today?" she asked. She emphasized the word "pigment" hoping the new apprentice would notice that she knew what it was.

"One of the reds," he replied. "This one is easy to grind into a powder."

"It must not be from a rock then," said Maria, showing off her knowledge. "Those are hard to grind."

Abraham grinned. "Do you want to grind up this one?"

She nodded, bouncing on her toes.

Abraham handed the mortar and pestle to her. "Don't get your nose too close to it."

"Why not?" Maria frowned and looked at Abraham.

"Just don't do it." He made a face.

She immediately leaned down to the rim of the mortar bowl and inhaled. She jerked back and grabbed her nose. "Eeew, that stinks!"

"Trust a girl not to listen," said Johann with a half-smile on his face.

Maria frowned at Johann.

"I'll bet you did the same thing," said Abraham.

Johann frowned and went back to his painting.

Maria looked down into the stone bowl she held. "What is this?"

"Cochineal," Abraham said. "They're insects. Dried insects."

"And paint is made from these stinky insects?"

Abraham nodded.

Maria leaned away as she finished grinding the dried insects into powdered pigment. Other than this cochineal, she loved the aromas of the different paints, thinners, varnishes, and ink. Some smelled rather like dirt; some were sharp. Studio scents were quite different from those of the house.

The smells in the Merian publishing house were different, too, mostly the vegetable oils and soot used to make ink. This was Wednesday afternoon, about the only time she could visit her half-brother, Caspar Merian. He was the only one of her older half-siblings who had anything to do with her.

Her eyes were glued to the strokes Caspar made

with his pointed engraving tool on the smooth, shiny surface of a flat copper plate. The piece of copper was about 7"x12" and already had many lines carved into its surface. The picture slowly emerged. She watched as Caspar made long sweeping strokes and short, quick, straight ones. She noticed how curved lines helped to make the objects look more real.

CHAPTER 4

Maria longed for her own paints. Finally she could stand it no longer. There on a bench she noticed an open half shell with only a little bit of dried green paint in it. She quickly slipped it into a pocket of her dress. Nobody noticed.

When she left the studio, she puzzled over where to put it. Somewhere where Sara, Franciscus, and the others can't find it, she thought. Or Mama. But where? She thought of and discarded several places. I know, the attic! Nobody goes up there.

Slanted rays of sunlight shone through the windows; evening would soon come. She looked around when she reached the door to the attic stairs. Nobody in sight. She listened, then opened the door and quietly made her way up the stairs.

The only light came from one small window. Boxes and pieces of discarded furniture sat scattered around. A large wooden box close to the window looked useable. Maria took the shell out of her pocket and placed it on the box. She imagined herself here, painting in her own place.

Lost in her thoughts, she did not hear the city noises outside, the clip-clop of hooves, or the creaking of carriages. She did not hear other kids shouting as they ran down the street. But soon she noticed that there was no more sunlight on the table. She looked outside. It was almost dark. Reluctantly she turned and walked downstairs to join the rest of the family.

The days passed, and Maria added to the items in her collection. She slipped each one into her pocket and later took it upstairs. After shells of dried paint came a brush and some discarded pieces of paper and parchment.

Finally she began working in the attic, remembering how her stepfather and his students held the brush, how much paint they loaded onto the brush before making their strokes, how they blended colors. She copied pictures of flowers, learning the distinctive shape and colors of each one.

One day when Maria was ten years old, she decided that she was ready to do more than copy pictures. She waited for the darkness of evening. Quietly she opened the door and slipped out into the night. The full moon provided enough light for her to see easily. She held her breath, but heard no sound from the house. She tiptoed into a count's nearby garden, and made her way over to a red and white tulip she had seen, the unusual one. She picked it, turned and hurried home.

Maria liked painting from a real flower instead of a picture of a flower. She decided to get a different tulip and paint that one, too. She slipped outside and went to the count's garden again. She reached for her chosen flower. Just as she picked it a strong hand gripped her shoulder and spun her around. She now faced an angry man.

Still clutching the tulip, she was escorted home where the count knocked on the door. Her stepfather answered. When he saw Maria held firmly in the count's grip, his expression changed to puzzlement. The count explained, in no uncertain terms, why he was there.

This was a serious theft. Not so many years before, one tulip bulb sold for more than the yearly income of a wealthy merchant. Maria Merian had no idea of the cost of those tulips. All she knew was that the count was furious. Her stepfather was not exactly happy, either.

"Why did you take the tulip, Maria?"

"Because I wanted to paint it," she replied through her tears. "I liked painting the other one, looking at a real tulip instead of just a picture, and I wanted to do another one."

Several seconds ticked by in silence. Finally the count spoke again. "I want to see this painting you have done," he said.

A few minutes later Maria slowly walked back into the room, the painting of the red and white tulip gripped tightly in her shaking hands. Tears shimmered in her eyes.

She handed the painting to the count, then

looked down. Nobody said anything. She sniffed. The count and her stepfather both stared at the lovely painting this ten-year old girl had made. Finally the count spoke.

"As payment for taking my tulip," he said, "I will keep this painting."

The following day Jacob called Maria to him. He looked very serious. "Maria, would you like to have lessons in drawing and painting?"

She looked up. Her eyes grew wide. "Really?"

"Really," he said.

Maria now looked forward to whole afternoons in the studio on Wednesdays and Saturdays. She was now included in the lessons her stepfather taught. But her mother had other plans.

"You must learn how to run a household," her mother said. She kept Maria busy cooking, cleaning, sewing, mending, keeping accounts, learning about the different herbs used for healing, and more. "No man wants a wife who cannot do these things," her mother said repeatedly. Maria preferred to spend her time in the studio.

"Painting is not going to get you a husband," snapped her mother.

At supper one evening Jacob announced that Johann would leave them. "I have taught him all I can. He will now travel around Europe, studying with other master artists, the last step in training to become a master artist, himself."

Maria speared a piece of meat with her fork. "I'd like to travel and become a master artist, too."

"But you're a girl," said Franciscus with a snort.

"Girls can't do that."

Maria sighed, and looked away. Something else girls can't do.

Soon her stepfather began making plans to leave for Utrecht. It was a long trip of 252 miles, but he still had a business there. More and more often he was gone from home, leaving Maria's mother alone with the children. With her stepfather gone, there would be no more art lessons and her mother would keep her extra busy with that dreaded housework.

"When will you come back?" she asked

"I don't know," he replied. "But don't worry, I have asked Abraham to continue teaching you while I'm gone."

A big smile lit up her face. She would still be able to paint, after all.

CHAPTER 5

Even the air danced with excitement. Gusts of wind picked up loose bits of paper, cloth, and leaves, spun them around and dropped them farther down the streets. The words "trade fair" bounced around in the breeze. Everywhere Maria heard people discussing the fair—on the way to school, at the market, going to and from church, everywhere. It seemed like everyone in the whole city was getting ready for the fair. Maria whirled around, her arms outstretched. "The fair is coming, the fair is coming," she chanted.

She saw "room available" signs popping up in house windows, which meant those people would rent out a room during the fair. Carpenters busy with their saws, hammers and hand forged nails, built extra storage buildings in the Römerberg, the largest market square in town. People unloaded boxes and bundles from wagons and carriages, then carried them into rented spaces inside those buildings. These temporary storage spaces were connected in a long row, and would come down once the fair was over.

"You know those little buildings they are putting up in the Römerberg?" Maria asked Caspar during a visit to the publishing house. "Why are the stone plaques at each door so plain? They have only the outline of an animal on them."

"Well," he answered, "they are made for the merchants who don't speak German. Those simple animal outlines help them find their rented places."

Maria agreed that was a good idea.

Later as she walked through the Römerberg she saw some newly arriving merchants. They were each presented with a large Welcome Pretzel. I'd like one of those, she thought. She could well imagine how good they must taste. A pretzel that big just has to be scrumptious!

On the first day of the trade fair it seemed like the entire city was up early. People rushed from one place to another.

"Is there a puppet show?" asked Sara.

"Are there any dancing monkeys?" asked Fredericus.

"I want to play the lottery at the Katharinen Gate," said Maria's mother. "Perhaps I'll win a nice silver piece for the house."

Besides the dancing, fireworks, singing, and unusual animals, there were also unusual, exotic things to see. There were furs and jewelry from other lands, and new inventions on display. New fabrics could also be seen at the Leinwandhaus.

Also, because Frankfurt was famous as a book printing city, there were many, many, new books. The trade fair was an important place to find new scientific books, essays and other educational books, all written in Latin.

The hustle, bustle, and excitement would continue until the last day when the trade fair flag was taken down and the bells of the city rang to signal the end of the fair. Then the merchants would pack up and leave, until the next time six months later.

CHAPTER 6

When she was thirteen, Maria's stepfather's brother gave her some tiny, black, hairy worms. Silkworms. They were the ones whose cocoons were unwound to make the thread used to make silk cloth. Because they were useful, people did not fear them.

"What do they eat?"

"Mulberry leaves. They eat a lot, and you will have to gather fresh leaves every day."

Two weeks later she sighed. They really did eat a lot! She had just returned from picking more leaves. The little silkworm caterpillars ate constantly. She watched, fascinated, as they grew bigger and shed the old, outgrown skin—five times. She painted small pictures showing how they changed. She also wrote notes about what she observed.

The black silkworms gradually changed color

until they were all white and lost all their hairs. Then they spun their cocoons and became still.

Patiently she waited to find out what happened next. She checked the cocoons often and kept fresh mulberry leaves ready. Three weeks later she noticed the end of one cocoon had a grayish spot. Then that spot wiggled, gradually protruding outward. Suddenly, a bit of black broke through. She grabbed her journal and began writing down the changes as she saw them.

Two black dots. She kept her eyes glued to those two black dots. And then there were two white legs waving around She watched whatever it was wiggle and twist, working to come out. Every time it rested, it seemed to slide back in a little. But with each spurt of activity it emerged farther. Soon she could see the segmented body. The front legs grabbed the strands holding the cocoon to the box and used them to help pull itself out. Now it was free. A cream-colored moth wiggled its small wet wings, then sat still. Amazing!

She continued watching. Gradually the wings expanded and dried. The light colored wings with small dark veins running to the edges matched the body.

Maria put fresh mulberry leaves near the little moth, but it did not eat. More of these moths with the fuzzy black antennae emerged. They all were active but stayed close to each other.

She noticed that some of them laid tiny eggs on the mulberry leaves. The moths still did not eat, and within a week they all died. Two weeks later tiny, black, furry silkworms hatched from the eggs, and the whole process started over again.

Did other caterpillars do this, too? There was no one she could ask.

Since Maria preferred drawing outside from nature, she was already in the habit of roaming the fields and meadows. Now when she was out she looked for caterpillars. She brought them home in little boxes or bags. She did this secretively at first, not wanting her mother to know that she was bringing Devil's worms home.

The first caterpillars she found would not eat the mulberry leaves she brought. They soon died. Then she brought home a caterpillar on a stalk of the plant where she found it. It continued eating all the leaves of that stalk. But it would not eat mulberry leaves. She went back to the plant where she found the caterpillar and brought home more of those leaves. The caterpillar ate them. Through trial and error she discovered that she must have the correct kind of plant for the different caterpillars to eat. If she had the wrong kind of leaves, they died.

Fascinated, Maria eagerly watched each caterpillar through the whole process as it transformed into a butterfly or moth.

Maria stepped into her stepfather's studio. Johann Graff, the oldest of the apprentices, had been gone for two years. Abraham sorted through a stack of drawings and watercolor paintings, laying a few to one side. Her stepfather carefully placed rolled canvases into a box.

"Make sure you have all of your personal things ready for tomorrow," said Jacob.

Abraham looked up and nodded. "I will be ready."

"Ready for what?" asked Maria.

"I'm going to Utrecht with your stepfather," said Abraham.

"What?" Her eyes got big. She put a hand up to her mouth.

"It's time for me to go, Maria. I have learned all that Jacob has to teach me. Now I must study with another master artist."

"Just like Johann," she said,

"Ja, just like Johann. I, too, am now a journeyman artist."

"And you will also become a master artist."

"I have another five years of study. After that I will paint my masterpiece. Then, if the guild decides I am good enough, yes, I will be a master artist."

Maria took a deep breath, sighed heavily, and left the room. Once again, she knew that there would never be such an opportunity for her. Women, no matter how talented or hard working, were not allowed to become master artists.

The next morning after Jacob and Abraham left Maria walked into the studio. No sounds. No movement. No life. She turned around and went back to her caterpillars and her research.

Soon her attic secret was out. Her mother definitely did not approve! "No husband will have those filthy creatures in his house!" But Maria's curiosity was so strong she kept on bringing caterpillars home to watch, paint and write about. It was the only way she had to find answers to her questions.

Maria also spent many hours, whether she wanted to or not, learning the skills considered necessary to be a wife. Still, her mother was worried about her.

"Why do you even want to be around those nasty Devil's worms?" she asked. "No man will want you for a wife if you continue with those creatures."

Maria had no answer that satisfied her mother.

When he was home, Jacob continued to encourage her in her artwork. He also began working on something new. He sat and wrote every day. Jacob wrote a book about painting for students. Maria became intrigued with the idea of writing and illustrating a book. She was eager to see his finished product. The day the books arrived from the printers she rushed into the workroom.

"Here," said Jacob, handing her a copy. "This one is yours to keep."

CHAPTER 7

Maria, now sixteen, spent as much time as possible in her stepfather's studio. She learned flower painting and composition from him, and helped with the studio work. She was busy grinding a small piece of malachite into powder with a mortar and pestle when a young man walked into the room.

"Johann!" said Jacob, rising to greet his former apprentice. "How are you?"

Maria went back to grinding. When she looked up she saw Johann glance at her.

Johann and Jacob continued talking. A few minutes later Johann picked up a small stack of flower paintings done in watercolor and looked at each of them.

"Those are Maria's paintings," said her stepfather.

Johann studied them more closely. "They're

quite good."

Maria smiled...until she heard the low, muttered "for a girl."

She left the studio.

A few days later Johann visited again. He came straight to the point. "I hear that you like those strange caterpillar creatures. And that you keep them in the house. Is that true?"

She nodded.

"Good Lord, why?"

"It's the only way I can study them."

His jaw dropped slightly. He frowned, and left.

On another visit Johann came into the studio as Maria signed a painting. He walked over to look. His brows drew together.

"You've signed it 'M. S. Merian,'" he said.

"Ja." She looked at him. Her mouth turned down. "Is something wrong with that?"

"But isn't your last name Marell?"

"No, Jacob is my stepfather."

"Then who is your father?"

"Matthäus Merian, the elder," she said. "Matthäus the younger is my half-brother." She swished the brush in water to clean it.

Johann's eyes widened. He stared at Maria.

"Your...father...was...Matthäus Merian? The famous engraver and publisher?"

"Ja, that is so."

"Mein Gott!" He blinked several times. "You are Maria Merian."

She gave him an exasperated look. "I told you that." She wiped her brush and placed it handle down in a jar full of other brushes. "I must go.

There is housework to be done."

For a while Johann did not visit at all, then he came regularly. But if he did not see Maria the visit was quite short. Her mother noticed, and commented on it.

"It is time for you to find a husband. If you don't marry soon you may wind up being a spinster, an old maid. You need a man to take care of you. Johann seems to be interested. This could be your only chance."

Maria turned away with a pained expression.

After Johann's next visit Maria went into the kitchen to help her mother.

"Did you learn anything about him to help you make a decision?" asked her mother.

"Not really. He just talks about himself. I want to know if he understands my need to paint. And if he accepts the caterpillars."

"Oh, Liebchen, don't mention the caterpillars. Not now."

Maria frowned. She knew she would have to marry someone. If she didn't, she would become a burden to her stepfather. He would have to continue providing for her for the rest of his life. There was no brother or uncle who would take her in. She sighed deeply. Johann might well be her only choice.

In April the marriage banns were read in church for three Sundays. Then came the required civil ceremony at City Hall.

Eighteen-year-old Maria packed her clothes, hope chest, and household items. She carefully packed all the boxes and jars of caterpillars, cocoons and butterflies, along with the needed supply of leaves. She packed her books, parchment, paper, brushes, pigments, and other necessary art supplies. Twenty-eight-year old Johann had boxes of his own to add to the growing pile in their house. They were married on Saturday, May 16, 1665.

A week later, in the morning, Maria heard the church bells strike eight. She grabbed a basket and left to shop for the two of them.

It was already crowded at the market place. The farmers were there with their carts and baskets of fresh vegetables to sell. Chickens cackled. Voices filled the fresh morning air. A light breeze gently stroked Maria's face. She exchanged greetings with neighbors and visited with friends as she shopped.

Back home she took several small pieces of wood from the open space under the large stone slab where she did the cooking. She carefully placed the wood over the still-warm coals. Using a bellows, she forced air across the coals until they glowed red and burst into a small flame. She hung a copper pot from the long hook hanging above the fire. She added water from a bucket. While that began to heat she chopped and added chunks of meat. She chopped onions and carrots and tossed them in the pot, along with a few herbs. This was an easy meal to make, giving her time to spend with her caterpillars.

"What? You spent how much?" Johann shouted, throwing his arms up in the air. "For more books?"

Maria had taken advantage of a sale to acquire a

number of important books. She could use these books to continue her studies of flower and insect painting. While she preferred to observe and paint them from life, this was not possible in the winter. That was when she turned to books to see what other artists had done.

"It's too much," Johann fumed.

Maria said not another word, but silently vowed to find a way to earn money herself. That way Johann could not complain about her spending his money.

It wasn't long before she saw what she could do. Every girl started early preparing for marriage, collecting items to use in her future home.

Maria embroidered and sold handkerchiefs, tablecloths, linens, pillows, etc. to wealthy young ladies for their hope chests.

But embroidery took a lot of time. She needed a way to get the designs on the cloth faster. Paint was the answer. She could now make and sell items more quickly.

Johann could no longer complain about her spending his money for things she wanted.

CHAPTER 8

Soon Maria had more to think about.

A baby. Would it be a girl or boy? Her mother helped her plan for the baby's arrival. Together they made clothes, blankets, and other items Maria and the baby would need.

The weather grew colder. Maria was glad, for that meant the caterpillars were all in a resting stage. She did not have to go outside and collect leaves every day for hungry caterpillars. By spring when they were active again she would be used to caring for a baby and could include time for them again.

The baby came on a cold day in early January of 1668. Maria held her newborn daughter in her arms and smiled. "Hello, little one," she whispered.

On January 5 the family gathered around the baptismal font at church. The minister held the baby over the water and baptized her with the name Johanna Helena Graff.

Soon Maria was juggling the care of a new baby with the work of running a household, plus making and selling her embroidered and painted cloths. Johann was not doing nearly so much.

It seemed that the art patrons of Frankfurt sponsored or often bought only from the artists who were born there. Those artists got the good commissions. It was hard for Johann to compete.

"You don't have any trouble selling things because you were born here," he told Maria.

"But the commissions don't just come to me. I have to work to get people to buy. Are you doing that?"

"What are you saying, that I'm lazy?"

"No, I was pointing out that making a sale takes work. It doesn't just happen."

"But you are also a Merian, part of that well-known family of artists. I thought being connected to the Merians would help me...but it hasn't."

"What?" Maria stepped back. "Is that why you married me?"

Johann didn't hear her. He was still talking. "I believe I can do better in Nürnberg, the city where I was born."

Johann made the decision to move to Nürnberg. Little Johanna was now two years old, old enough to travel. Moving day arrived, April 1, 1670.

Johann's relatives had found a house for them. Their travel papers were in order. They gathered their belongings, said goodbye to Maria's family, and climbed in the horse-drawn coach. The driver flicked the reins, and with a lurch they were on their way. It would be a long, bumpy ride, first on the cobblestone streets and later on rough dirt roads.

Maria wondered what Nürnberg would be like and hoped she'd like it there. Would there be new kinds of caterpillars? She looked forward to not having to make and sell things. Was this how a journeyman felt as he left to learn new things?

They quickly reached the bridge that crossed the Main River to Sachsenhausen. From there the road followed the bends and curves of the river. They traveled through the countryside and small towns. Their only stops were to change horses, and to eat.

The day's journey ended that evening in the small town of Seligenstadt. They had traveled less than twenty-five miles.

Early the next morning they climbed back in the coach to continue their journey. By late afternoon low mountains appeared in the distance.

On the third day of their journey they followed the river south through the towns of Klingenberg and Miltenberg. They suddenly heard a loud crack, and came to an immediate stop. One of the axles broke. They got out of the carriage and waited while the axle was replaced. Then they resumed their journey on to Würzburg.

On Monday, April 7, they left Würzburg and traveled away from the river. Low, grey clouds gathered. It started to rain. The horses slowed to a walk as the road became muddy. They struggled to lift their feet up out of the mud to take the next step. Little Johanna became cranky. She squirmed and wiggled. She cried. She pushed at those next to her. It was a long, miserable day. Finally they stopped at Kitzingen, glad to be able to get out and move around.

"How long will it be before we reach Nürnberg?"

"That depends on the weather," said Johann.

They all groaned when it started raining again. It became even more difficult for the horses. The slick road caused the carriage to slide. When they stopped in a small town for the night, Maria didn't even ask where they were.

On their last day of travel they woke up to sunshine. Their spirits lifted. This day had to be better than the previous two.

"There it is," said Johann. "Nürnberg." They saw the many tall spires, towers, steeples, and bright red roofs of the city. A castle stood at the north edge of town, on a hilltop.

Maria was excited. She was also a bit worried. She shifted in her seat and wondered if Johann's family would like her. She smoothed her hair.

The carriage stopped at a closed city gate. They handed their papers to the guard for inspection. He returned their papers, then let down the drawbridge. The driver flicked the reins and the carriage moved. The horses walked sedately across the wooden drawbridge and into the crowded street.

The carriage stopped at one side of an open cobblestone square bustling with activity. They stepped out and looked around. "We are home," said Johann.

CHAPTER 9

It was time to explore this new city. Maria took Johanna's hand and together they walked uphill along the Burgstrasse. As the street became steeper they walked more slowly, breathing heavily. Johanna hung back until her mother picked her up and carried her. When they reached the street called Am Ölberg the limestone rock cliff rose abruptly higher, up to the castle. Maria set Johanna down and stopped to catch her breath. They turned left where the ground was almost level and followed the inside of the wall surrounding the city. There were places where houses were built up against the wall, but there were gardens, too.

Gardens. Good places to search for caterpillars. Would there be different ones here? The chrysalises she had brought when they moved would soon become butterflies. She needed new caterpillars to study.

When they reached a city gate, Maria looked back towards town, searching for the twin spires of St. Sebaldus Church, near their home. Using the spires as a guide, she and Johanna headed back.

At home, Maria laid wood on the large, waist-high stone in the kitchen and used the bellows to help get the fire going. She heated food in a pot which she swung over the fire. After they ate she settled Johanna for a nap and turned her attention to more unpacking.

Johann returned home, avidly talking about some friends he had seen. "We will meet again tomorrow morning at four," he said.

"What? In the middle of the night?"

"No," Johann replied, "in the morning. At four o'clock."

"But that's in the middle of the night!"

"No it isn't," protested Johann. "It's four hours after sunrise."

Maria frowned as she thought about this. If the sun came up at six, then four hours later would be ten. "But isn't that ten o'clock?" she asked.

"Ach," said Johann. "We tell time differently here in Nürnberg. Here we count from sunup and from sunset, starting with 'one' each time."

Maria was still puzzled. "So you are meeting your friends in daylight? Before the mid-day meal?"

"Ja, that is so."

For several weeks Maria found this new way of telling time very confusing. It meant that four o'clock was not at exactly the same time every day because the sun did not rise at exactly the same time every day. And it meant that in the dark of winter she would have to get used to hearing the church bells strike one or two o'clock a few hours before it was time to go to bed! For someone who was used to the clocks chiming thirteen, fourteen, fifteen, all the way to twenty-four chimes at midnight, this was downright strange.

Later that day Johann took Maria and little Johanna to meet his family. Maria looked forward to meeting them, but she also felt anxious. She smoothed her hair with her fingers.

"Don't mention caterpillars," Johann said just before they went in.

The visit went well...until Maria mentioned the many gardens in town and how she looked forward to searching for caterpillars in them. The atmosphere instantly changed. She watched everyone's expression change, their lips tightening in disapproval, including Johann's.

CHAPTER 10

A few days later Maria and Johann were each working on their own project in their studio. Afternoon sunshine streamed in the windows. Johann took a copper plate and laid it on the table next to his drawing. Maria moistened her brush just enough to lift the last of the yellow pigment from its shell container. There was barely enough to finish the last yellow flower petal in her painting. She looked up.

"When does the paint supplier come again?" she asked.

"I heard that he's expected sometime next week," replied Johann.

"Good. I'm now out of saffron yellow. And I need more azurite." She knew she had enough cochineal since only small amounts were needed at a time. She should check her supply of other pigments.

Some things used to make pigments she could get locally. The items they had to buy included the blue rocks azurite and lapis lazuli, the green rock malachite, and cinnabar for a red.

The next few weeks were busy ones. Maria was introduced to many people. Johann met more old friends and acquaintances, making contacts for his business. He was often gone most of the day sketching houses, businesses, and street scenes around town.

Maria enjoyed the large number of gardens both inside and outside of the city walls. There were well over a hundred, including vegetable gardens, kitchen herb gardens, and flower gardens. Plenty of places to look for caterpillars.

Maria took Johanna to see the hyacinths newly in bloom. They admired the many florets on the otherwise bare stalks. The tall, straight leaves grew on separate stalks around the flowers.

"A caterpillar!" cried Johanna. She pointed to the fuzzy creature with small white spots on its bands of black. She squealed when she touched the topside of the fuzz, but jerked her hand back when the caterpillar rolled up and fell off the leaf.

At home Maria wrote down where they found the caterpillar, described it, and then made a drawing of it.

In April she found a fuzzy caterpillar on a buttercup. It was black with long yellow stripes. Another one just like it sat on a dandelion. She scooped them both up and took them home, along with buttercup and dandelion leaves for food.

Whenever she touched either one of these caterpillars it rolled up into a tight circle.

In early May, Maria picked some of the herb chervil to use as flavoring in butter, salads, and sauces. In that garden she found a light blue-green caterpillar with long white stripes down its smooth segmented body. This one didn't move much, she noticed. And when it did, it moved rather slowly. It joined the others in her house.

On another day she grabbed a large basket, left the house and walked downhill. The sunshine was warm, but the air was still chilly. The sun played peek-a-boo among the gray clouds overhead. Maria hoped to buy asparagus at the market; this being the season that farmers brought in those fresh, delicious, long white stalks.

She entered the busy market near the Schönebrunnen, the beautiful fountain, with its sixty-foot tall spire. She checked the fresh fish to her right, then joined other women feeling and smelling the vegetables before making their choices. She bought turnips, radishes, lettuce, kale, and asparagus. Asparagus! She could almost taste it already and began planning the noon meal.

But her footsteps slowed as she headed home.

CHAPTER 11

Maria found herself longing for Frankfurt. She started making comparisons. She pictured in her mind the three buildings that made up the Römer (the city hall), each with its stair-stepped façade. And the large, open market space in front. Here there was just a street in front of the city hall. There was no way here in Nürnberg to have those big, wonderful celebrations in front of their city hall. Not as good as in Frankfurt, she thought.

The church bells rang and she looked up, comparing the position of the sun in the sky with the chimes of the bells. "What an idiotic way of telling time. In Frankfurt they know how to do it right!"

And the Pegnitz, such a little river, was certainly nothing like the river Main. She visualized the big ships in Frankfurt with their masts and sails, tied up at the docks. She saw again in her mind the ships being loaded and unloaded, all the activity. There was nothing like that here. She sighed.

The next morning Maria listened to the chatter of the neighbor women as she stood in line waiting for her turn to draw water from the well. They gossiped about their families, friends, and others. They discussed who was sick, who had visitors, and anything else they had heard.

She knew very few of the people they talked about. How different it all was. She thought of the many people she knew in Frankfurt and wondered what they were doing. She longed to see, touch, and speak with them again.

Maria stayed busy to keep that ache from growing. She cleaned house, washed and mended the clothes, and spent time with her active young daughter. She gathered fresh leaves for her growing number of caterpillars, watched them, took notes, and made sketches and paintings of their changes.

In June, a moth emerged, its wide antennae marking it as a night flier. The color surprised her. Who would have thought that such a black caterpillar would turn out to be a bright white and yellow moth!

The smooth, light blue-green caterpillar with the long white stripes, the one that moved so slowly, became a copper-green moth. As a moth it moved as slowly as it had when a caterpillar.

Maria stayed so busy with her own thoughts and activities that she scarcely noticed what Johann was or was not doing. That was brought to her attention when Johann complained loudly. It was like

Frankfurt all over again. He talked with many people, but received few commissions. Maria sighed. Once again she would have to help support the family. But this time, with a young daughter to care for, she had even less time to make items to sell. She would have to find another way to use her talents. What could she do?

The answer came to her as she explained to Johanna how to wash her hands before eating. "You wash only the first two fingers and your thumb, like this," Maria said. "So we don't waste water. The more water we use, the more trips I have to make to the well."

Johanna nodded and carefully washed just the first two fingers and thumb of each hand.

Maria smiled. That was her answer: Teaching.

She would teach young ladies how to paint and how to embroider—five or six girls together at once. That would take less time, and she would earn more money. She called her school the Jungfern Companie, the Company of Young Maidens.

Starting a school for girls was very unusual for a woman. There was no law, however, to keep her from doing just that. She inquired as to which patrician families had young girls who would be interested in taking her classes. Her school became a reality.

"Johann, I have news."

"What kind of news?" he asked.

"I started a school for young women, to teach them embroidery and watercolor painting. Classes begin in two weeks."

"How did you do that?" He shook his head.

"This is not Frankfurt." Johann rubbed the back of his neck. "Again you find a way. But I...."

"You look unhappy, Johann. I thought you'd be glad to know that we will have more income."

"Well, ja, but...." He sighed and left the room.

Maria prepared for her classes. The students could easily get thread to use for their embroidery. But what about paint pigments? She decided to make and sell the pigments to her students. She also decided to make her own patterns for the girls to use. The first pattern was a bouquet of flowers with a blue ribbon tied around the stems. She then made several others.

At this point Maria became a full-fledged businesswoman.

In early spring she took her students into gardens and fields. She felt it was important to draw and paint from living things. (She was also then able to search for caterpillars and gather needed leaves.)

The Jungfern Companie was a success.

Maria, like other artists, had her own secret formula for paint and colors. Her fabric paints were unique because the colors did not run or fade when the cloth was wet. Anything she painted could be washed. This impressed the Princess of Baden-Baden so much that she bought a tablecloth from Maria, and even washed it in public to show that the colors were water resistant.

Another unique quality of Maria's painted fabrics was that they looked as good from the back as they did on the front. That is why Prince Louis

William of Baden-Baden commissioned a special piece from Maria.

"He wants what?" asked Johann as he raised his eyebrows.

"He wants me to paint the inside of a tent."

"A tent," replied Johann. "And what, exactly, does he want you to paint on this tent?"

"Plants, flowers, and butterflies," replied Maria.

"He wants plants, flowers, and butterflies." Johann shook his head. "Isn't he a General in the Imperial Army? Doesn't he know that these will show on the outside of his tent as well?"

"Ja, he knows that," replied Maria. "That's why he commissioned me to paint them."

Johann left the room muttering "plants, flowers, and butterflies," still shaking his head.

CHAPTER 12

Joachim van Sandrart, a famous artist, moved to Nürnberg in 1673, and became friends with Johann and Maria Graff. The following year, Herr von Sandrart became the director of the new Art Academy in town. Even though Maria knew the director, she could not study there. Females were not allowed.

In 1675 Joachim von Sandrart published a book which included biographies of artists that he knew personally. Johann Graff was mentioned, but much more was written about Maria. As part of her biography von Sandrart mentioned the copper engravings she made as patterns for students. He pointed out her "...specialization in painting flowers, fruits, birds, and especially insects which she observed herself."

"Why don't you publish these patterns, Frau

Graff?" asked her students. Other friends encouraged her to publish as well.

Maria sat down to figure out how much it would cost to publish a book. The copper engravings were already done. The pages would be about 5 1/2 inches by 8 1/4 inches in size. That would cost less than a book with larger pages. The printed pages would have to be sent to a bookbinder...

She chose twelve of her floral engravings. Every one of her pictures had a butterfly and/or another insect. In the preface she wrote that the book was for people to copy and use as patterns for painting and embroidery. She also said the book was for the pleasure of all lovers of art.

She did not want the printed, hand-colored copies of this book to have those dark black outlines made by the engravings. So she began experimenting. She discovered how to make prints in a way so that the outlines were lighter and softer. They even appeared to blend in with the paint. She inked the copper plate, placed a sheet of parchment on the plate, and ran it through the printing press. She then immediately placed another sheet on top of the wet print and ran both of them through the press again. After the printing was finished she hand painted each page...for each book!

Johann, who published this pattern book, was delighted with its success.

Maria went back to collecting caterpillars, watching them, and taking notes.

Johann was seldom home. When Maria noticed this and tried to talk to him about it, he quickly dismissed it, saying he was busy. Maria could not figure out what was wrong, so she again focused on her butterflies and caterpillars.

While other artists talked about the wonderful creations of God, they never mentioned caterpillars and butterflies as God's creations. Maria would remedy that. She would write a book herself. She would show what she had learned through her own experience so other people would understand that these insects were also God's creations. She made a very important decision to show the entire life cycle of the moth or caterpillar on the plant that was its food source. This had never been done before.

She sorted through her paintings and notes to decide which ones to use. Definitely that beautiful yellow caterpillar that had those funny tufts sticking up on its back, with one long, bright red feathery-looking thing at one end. It was a very timid caterpillar, she remembered. As soon as it felt or sensed anything, it rolled into a ball and remained very still.

She thought about other illustrations she could make. She had a lot of notes and small drawings and paintings to work from. She decided not to tell Johann about this new idea. With Johanna now in school Maria would have more time for painting. And with more time she could even create another pattern book. That would bring in money while she worked on the caterpillar book. She would tell Johann about the second pattern book.

Johann smiled when Maria told him about the second pattern book. He would, of course, publish this book. Once again he was home more.

The second pattern book, published in 1677, was

also a success.

CHAPTER 13

In late January 1678, a second child, Dorothea Maria Graff, was born.

Maria's mother and stepfather came. Her mother came to help, her stepfather came because women were not allowed to travel alone. Ten-year-old Johanna and her grandmother took over the duties of the household since new mothers were supposed to stay in bed for a month after the birth of the baby.

On February 2 the family, bundled up against the cold, walked downhill to St. Sebaldus Church a short distance away. They returned home after the short baptism ceremony for baby Dorothea.

"Johanna, would you put more wood in the stove, please?" asked her grandmother. Many people would come soon to congratulate Maria and Johann, and to see the baby.

Johanna glanced at the tall, square, green

ceramic heating stove sitting flush against the wall on her way out. When she returned carrying the wood, she walked past the door to the living room and on down the hall to a little door set low in the wall. She opened this door and added the wood piece by piece to the fire in the stove. Now the room would stay warm for visitors.

A month to stay in bed was a long time for Maria, who had been constantly working on something, and soon she could stand it no longer. It wasn't long before her mother found her in the studio holding a paintbrush.

"You know you shouldn't be out of bed this soon," chided her mother.

"I know, Mama, but I need to finish this painting," Maria replied. She applied the tip of the paintbrush to the sheet of vellum and left a delicate, curved trail of shimmering blue.

Her mother sighed and turned away.

Her stepfather appeared in the doorway. "There you are."

Both women looked up.

"What are you working on, Liebchen?" Jacob asked as he walked over to Maria.

"I'm painting a butterfly." She smiled and looked down at her work. "What I'm painting right now is the circle on each wing that looks like the eyes of a peacock's tail—this lovely blue, yellow, white, purple, and black. The rest of the wing is bright red, except for a couple of white spots here." She pointed to a pattern of five spots on the upper wing.

Below the butterfly was a caterpillar on a plant

leaf.

"And this caterpillar?" asked Jacob.

"That is the caterpillar that becomes this butterfly."

Her mother looked more closely at the painting, at the segmented black caterpillar with many small white dots on its body. It also had black spines sticking out from its back and sides.

"That ugly thing? Becomes this butterfly?"

"Ja," said Maria. "But first the butterfly lays tiny green eggs on this plant. It has to be this particular plant because its leaves are the food for the little caterpillars when they emerge from the eggs."

"How do you know this?" asked her mother.

"It's what I've seen, Mama. All those caterpillars I brought home I've fed and watched the changes. I made notes, drawings, and small paintings of it all."

"So they really don't ooze up out of the ground." Johanna Marell considered what that meant. "Then they are not the Devil's work."

"No, Mama. They are all examples of God's wonderful creations."

Perhaps at this point her mother realized just how important her daughter's "messing around with caterpillars" really was. She was proving to everybody that these small creatures really were God's work.

"How many of these paintings are you going to do?"

"Fifty. I've decided to publish a book."

Now that was something!

The coach stopped in the open square of the

Milchmarkt. It was time. Maria's mother and stepfather needed to go back home to Frankfurt.

The cold wind slashed across their unprotected faces, hurrying the older couple to the open door of the coach. Jacob helped his wife into the carriage, then climbed in and sat beside her. The driver added their bags to those already on top of the coach before settling onto the driver's seat. He flicked the reins and the four horses moved forward.

"Have a safe journey," said Maria. She and her daughter Johanna waved as they watched the coach head up the hill and turn left toward the city gate. They hurried back into the house to the warmth of the big green stove.

Johann and Maria saw less and less of each other. She complained he was always out. He complained she was always busy. "Even a new baby doesn't keep you from thinking of those awful caterpillars. Now you're even making paintings of them. And what are those engravings?"

"I'm making a book, Johann. A book showing the transformations of caterpillars into butterflies."

"And who will buy this book," he asked. "You do not have ready buyers like you have for your pattern books. Young ladies will not want to make embroideries of caterpillars."

"This will be a natural history book, Johann."

"But you are not a naturalist!"

"I may not have studied at the university, but I have spent my life studying these caterpillars. I know what they eat. I have raised them and watched all the changes they go through. I have seen them shed their skin when they grow too big for it. I have watched them turn themselves into that stage they go through before coming out as a butterfly or moth. I have seen the butterflies lay tiny eggs, and have watched the little caterpillars emerge from those eggs and start the cycle all over again."

Johann reminded her that natural history books were written in Latin, a language she did not know.

"I can't write in Latin since girls aren't taught Latin, you know that."

Johann stepped back and shook his head. "Well, no scholar will read your book. They will not be interested in your silly fascination with caterpillars."

"My book is for everybody, Johann, not just scholars. No one will be excluded from reading and learning from my book."

Johann made a face. "Your other books, your pattern books are something useful for women. They help women occupy their time in ways fitting for a woman. This book does not." He shook his index finger at her. "The people who matter, those we depend on for commissions, they will laugh at you."

Johann strode to the door. "I do not want to be involved with this. You need to get this idea out of your head." He left.

Maria stared after him.

CHAPTER 14

Johann mentioned his wife's silly idea to Andreas Knortzen, a printer in Nürnberg. Knortzen, however, was interested in the book. He thought there was a possibility for good sales, especially since he worked with David Funken who was a bookseller in both Frankfurt and Leipzig. That would expand the distribution of her books outside of Nürnberg. Johann was now interested. A wider distribution of her books would mean more money.

At home Johann told Maria that he had changed his mind and would help her with this new book. Maria could now work without Johann getting mad at her.

Finished. Maria leaned back and stretched. That was the last of the comments about the caterpillars and butterflies. All of the copper engravings were done. Her book was ready. She gave it all to Johann to take to the printers.

Two weeks passed. Maria was restless. It was still winter and very cold. There were no leaves to gather, no caterpillars to care for, no new butterflies or moths to paint, no book needing her attention.

No book? Hmm...

The girls of the Jungfern Companie could use more embroidery and painting patterns.

She began drawings for a new pattern book. She was busy with another flower pattern when she heard footsteps in the hall.

"It's here!" came a shout.

Johann entered the studio and handed Maria a leather bound book. "A brand new copy of your caterpillar book," he said.

Maria held the volume in her hands. She felt its weight. She inhaled the smell of the leather cover. She ran her fingers along the shiny gilt edges of the vellum pages.

She carefully opened the book and looked at her name on the title page: "...self-published by Maria Gräffin, legitimate daughter of Matthäus Merian the Elder." She smiled. Maria had played a word game with her last name. Graf was the word for the title of "Count." Gräffin was the feminine form of Graf, the word for "Countess."

She read the German title out loud. "Der Raupen Wunderbare Verwandelung und Sonderbare Blumennahrung." The Caterpillar's Wonderful Metamorphosis and Special Plant Food.

She read the poem at the beginning of the book titled Caterpillar Song, written by her friend, Pastor

Christoph Arnold. She especially liked the last verse where Pastor Arnold mentioned how the caterpillar changed from what looked like a dead cocoon into the new life of a butterfly. He compared that change with the hope that people would also have a new life after death.

Johanna read the title of her mother's book. "What does metamorphosis mean?"

"It means changes like the changes a caterpillar goes through to become a butterfly. You know, when they stop eating and crawling and change into a form that just hangs there. And later a butterfly, or moth, comes out, completely different from when it was a caterpillar."

Johanna nodded.

The caterpillar book was shown at the Trade Fairs in Frankfurt and Leipzig. Soon many people talked about it, saying things like...

"Have you seen the book about caterpillars by Maria Gräffin?"

"Did you know that caterpillars eat plants?"

"Look at this! Here's the caterpillar that becomes this butterfly."

"Where does the caterpillar come from?"

"It comes from butterfly eggs. That's what Maria Gräffin says, right here, see?"

"She did the research herself. She really does know about this."

The natural philosophers, however (there was no word yet for science or scientists), at first did not take her work seriously. It was printed in German instead of Latin. And she was a woman. But she was becoming very well known. Finally the natural philosophers were won over. They had to admit that she had made new discoveries. She showed them a new view of nature. Her style of illustrations was new. Her methods of research were new. She even categorized the insects, dividing them into day fliers and night fliers.

"Mama? Are you finished with caterpillars now?" asked Johanna.

"Of course not," said Maria. "As soon as the weather is warmer we will look for new ones again." She looked up. "Why do you ask?"

"Oh, something I heard Papa say. He said that finally you should be able to give up chasing caterpillars now that you have published a book about them."

"As long as there are more caterpillars and butterflies out there, I will continue looking for them and studying them," her mother assured her.

In 1680 Maria completed another pattern book, the Third Collection of Flowers, which her husband published. Later that year he published all three books as one collection. That collection was known as the Neues Blumen Buch, the New Flower Book.

Maria's students often helped her look for caterpillars when they were outside painting. Some brought her caterpillars they found in other places. She even received a few caterpillars from acquaintances, too. Often those people did not include leaves with these insects, and these caterpillars died.

Maria expanded her searches. In 1681 she visited the famous maze near Kraftshof. In Augsburg she fished a caterpillar out of the moat to add to her collection.

Maria discovered another way to make money. Wealthy people were collectors of nature. Many of them had cabinets filled with their collections. That included mounted insects, which meant she could sell dried butterflies.

She didn't know how to dry and mount butterflies, but that did not stop her. She began experimenting. It did not all go smoothly. At first she damaged the wings while she worked with them. She learned to heat the point of a needle in a candle flame until the needle glowed hot before she stuck the hot needle through the body of a live butterfly, killing it instantly. This way the wings remained undamaged. She placed the butterfly on a piece of wood and carefully arranged the wings. It took up to four weeks for the insect to dry out.

But there was another problem she had to solve. Worms found the drying butterflies and quickly made a mess of them. Maria learned to place her drying butterflies in cloth bags coated in oil. The oil kept the worms out, and the cloth bags kept the dead butterflies safe while they dried. Only then were the mounted butterflies ready to sell.

CHAPTER 15

Maria set the letter from her mother on the small table next to her chair, and held Johanna close. She explained that Grandpa had died and Grandma needed their help. They would leave as soon as possible for Frankfurt.

Maria notified her students that she was leaving. She carefully packed all of her paints, brushes, notebooks, copper plates, engraving tools, embroidery supplies, and other necessary items. She helped her girls as the three of them packed their clothes.

Johann packed a smaller bag. He would travel with them, then come back after a few days.

It was a long journey. The landscape was bare since the trees had lost most of their leaves, and the crops had all been harvested. The crisp winds found their way into and through the carriage. The bundled up passengers snuggled into their lap robes for warmth.

A big lump formed in Maria's throat and she fought back a sob. Jacob was the only one who always believed in her. He never fussed about the caterpillars.

Six days later they arrived in Frankfurt. They left the carriage and walked to the house. The next few weeks were a whirlwind of activity. The funeral had been on Friday, November 11, 1681, before Maria had even received her mother's letter. But there was still much to be done, many things to sort through.

Jacob had left a large number of paintings and other artwork. Maria and her mother arranged for the sale of all of this art. Her mother needed the money. Without a husband she now had no income. Jacob had also left many debts. As soon as they paid one off, another surfaced. Unfortunately, after all the artwork was sold, there were still debts left to pay.

Once again Maria's family depended on her to provide for them. Once again she supplied paint pigments to her students in Nürnberg. She also started teaching a group of young girls in Frankfurt, and sold them the supplies they needed for their painting and embroidery.

In the spring Maria again searched for caterpillars. In the middle of May 1682 she spotted a large web with about seventy tiny black caterpillars. They were bunched together in a circle on the sloe hedges bordering a street. Together they looked like a round, black patch of velvet. Of course she took them back to the house to raise.

And each day she came back to those hedges to gather fresh leaves. Her daughters often went with her.

Dorthea was the now the one with questions.

"How can they eat so fast?"

"How do you know which caterpillar becomes which butterfly?"

"Why does a caterpillar shed its skin?"

"Do people ever shed their skin?"

"No, people don't have to shed their skin because our skin grows as we grow," replied her mother.

Maria found it easier to come back than she expected. Her mother no longer fussed about the caterpillars. Several times she had seen her mother peering intently in a box or jar. But as soon as her mother saw her, she gave some other reason for being there. And now that she worked on a second caterpillar book her mother often checked on her progress.

"What are you doing now?"

"This painting will show a night flier," said Maria. It will be this gray one." She showed her mother the small painting she was working from.

"That red there where the two wings meet, that looks almost like feathers," said her mother. "Does the caterpillar it comes from have any red on it?"

Maria shook her head. "It's a white caterpillar with odd shaped brown patches."

"So the butterfly does not always look similar to what it looked like as a caterpillar?"

Maria laughed. "No. I thought so when I began all this," she said, waving her hand at the boxes and jars. "I remember one very pretty caterpillar; I eagerly waited for the butterfly to emerge. I was positive it would be the most gorgeous one ever. It was such a disappointment. It came out all grayish-brown. Not a single bit of bright color."

Her mother nodded.

"Mama, are you going to use that bright red butterfly in your book?" asked Johanna one evening.

"Definitely," said her mother. "In fact, I'm drawing the caterpillar that goes with it right now."

Her daughter pointed to a small painting on the table. "This brown one with black spikes."

"That's right, the one we found in the pear tree."

As busy as Maria was, she still found time to write letters, especially to Caspar. She told him about her growing unhappiness with Johann. Each visit to was shorter than the previous one. Caspar was now the only member of her family who wrote to her. He had moved to northern Holland to live with a community of Labadists.

Her mother handed her a letter that had just come. It was from Caspar. She smiled as she opened the letter. Maria had asked him to tell more about life where he lived at Waltha Castle.

They lived simply, he said, and as a community tried to be as self-sufficient as possible. They raised crops in the fields surrounding the castle. They had a butcher, a tanner, a print shop, a weaving room, their own barber and doctor, a smithy and a shoemaker. Everyone was assigned a job, and there were classes for the children. Church services were held in a large dining hall, the same one where they all ate their meals together.

"Our life is plain," he wrote. "We wear plain clothing, nothing fancy. Here you and your mother will find security and acceptance."

He mentioned one more thing. A marriage in the Labadist religion was not recognized unless both husband and wife were Labadists.

Maria shared the letter with her mother. Here was a chance to solve their immediate problems. If they moved to the castle there would be no worries about money, food, or a place to stay. They would have no bills to pay. It sounded like everything they needed would be provided. Maria would no longer be responsible for everybody.

But who were these Labadists?

This small religious group, founded by Jean de Labadie, met in people's houses to study the Bible. They focused on living a simple life together and serving God. The community at Waltha Castle shared their possessions, work, and their meals. They took care of each other.

Johann would not want to be a part of this. That meant that to the Labadists she would no longer be married to Johann. A divorce in Nürnberg would be difficult for her to get, so joining the Labadists and moving to Waltha Castle seemed to be a solution for this problem, too.

CHAPTER 16

Maria, her mother, and her two daughters stood at the edge of the square with their belongings, waiting for the coach that would take them to Mainz. They listened to the clip-clop of horses' hooves on the cobblestones, and the wagons creaking as the people of Frankfurt went about their business.

A large coach, pulled by six horses, stopped in front of them. This was their coach. Once they climbed in they would definitely leave Frankfurt behind. Destination: Waltha Castle in northern Holland.

Two days later they reached Mainz where they would begin the next stage of their journey, by ship down the Rhein River.

They boarded the ship with the other passengers. There was a lot of activity as trunks and boxes of all sizes were lifted up and placed on deck. It seemed as though everyone was talking, now shouting back and forth between the passengers on the ship and the people on land. They watched as ropes were untied, and then they felt the gentle swaying movement as the ship left the shore. The city of Mainz became smaller and smaller.

Flat land soon gave way to hills gradually becoming higher and closer to the river.

"There are more castles on the river from Rüdesheim to Koblenz than in any other river valley in the world," said Hans, one of the passengers they met. "At the deepest and narrowest part of the river are dangerous reefs and rapids. And the Lorelei."

"What's the Lorelei?" asked Dorothea.

"The Lorelei sits on top of one very tall rock and sings. Some people say she lures sailors to their deaths with her singing."

"We have to pay close attention to the river there," said one of the crewmen. "The river makes a large turn to the right, and then quickly turns again to the left. If the crew were to try and look at the Lorelei their ship could easily crash on the rocks, and people could drown."

"Does she want people to die?" asked Dorothea.

"Maybe so," replied Hans. He puffed on his pipe. "Maybe so."

As they passed St. Goar, Hans pointed out a castle to Dorothea. "You'll like this one," he said. This castle belonged to Count Katzenelnbogen."

"Really?" She laughed. "Was he really called Cat's Elbow?"

"Ja. And so was his castle. Now it's just called

The Cat. And a smaller castle downriver is called The Mouse."

Dorothea giggled.

After Koblenz the Rhein River became wider as the land flattened out with the hills set back away from the river. They passed many more small villages.

The Siebengebirge (Seven Mountains) came into view. Maria watched for the Drachenfels. She recognized the Dragon Rock from an engraving her father had made long ago.

As the ship sailed farther north the land flattened out even more and the river widened. They could not travel as far in a day, now, because the wider river ran more slowly. Eventually they crossed into the Netherlands, and Maria and her family left the ship at one of the Dutch ports.

Once again they traveled by carriage.

In Leeuwerden Maria arranged transportation for the four of them plus their baggage to Wieuwert. From Wieuwert they headed into the countryside to Waltha Castle. They had been traveling an entire month. Maria had as much trouble sitting still as her youngest child, Dorothea, did.

The approach to the castle was by a long lane lined with a row of trees on each side. The trees leaned slightly toward each other, forming a green canopy overhead. A canal ran parallel with the lane on the right. Both the land and the canal ended at the castle gate. This was a very tall, arched wooden gate with a large column on each side. Tall, curved double doors were set in the arch. The left half of the double doors had a smaller door, people sized. It stood open as if expecting them.

CHAPTER 17

A small group of people greeted the family. Although they spoke Dutch, many words sounded a lot like German, so Maria and her family understood enough. One of the women showed them to their rooms. The others carried their trunks, boxes, and bundles.

Each room was plain and furnished simply. There were no pictures or decorations on the walls. A single window had shutters open to let in the light. There was a cabinet to hold their clothing, a small table, wooden chairs, and a bed.

Dorothea skipped over and tested the bed. She peeked under the wool blanket and checked the mattress—a sack, really—filled with straw, on a tight lattice work of rope. Dorothea also checked under the bed to make sure a chamber pot was there, in case she had to go to the bathroom during the night.

"I would like to see my brother," said Maria once she saw that all of their things were now in their rooms.

"Certainly. I will take you to him," replied the woman. "But first..." She saw the look on Dorothea's face and how she stood. "First, I will show you the nearest outhouse."

She led them outside and gestured towards a small wooden building on the other side of the canal. Dorothea ran across the little bridge and disappeared into the outhouse. When she rejoined them they went back into the castle to see Caspar.

"I'm so glad you're here," said Caspar. A big smile spread across his face. "It's been a long time."

"It has," agreed Maria. "It's so good to see you again." She motioned her daughters forward. "You will not recognize Johanna," she said. "She's all grown up at seventeen."

"You are right about that," said Caspar, reaching out to shake Johanna's hand. "The last time I saw you, you were quite little."

"And this is Dorothea, my younger daughter," said Maria. "She's seven."

Caspar reached out to Dorothea. "I have heard about you from your mother's letters. It's nice to finally meet you."

Dorothea shook his hand.

Caspar and Maria chatted awhile. Maria asked who owned the castle.

"The Sommelsdijk family owns the castle," said Caspar. "The three sisters, Anna, Maria, and Lucia, live here. Their brother, Cornelius, lives in

Suriname, South America. He is Governor there."

After a few more minutes Caspar said, "You must be tired from traveling, and curious about your new home. Go, rest, or look around. We will have plenty of time to talk now that you are here." He smiled.

The next few days were busy ones settling in, getting acquainted, and learning what was where. The castle complex was quite large. The main part of the castle was separated from the work area by an arched bridge over one of the canals. A smaller bridge led to some small gardens and other houses and cottages. Behind these was the laundry.

Later Maria found the silk spinning room, chicken house, and beer brewery. Also the barber shop, the chemist, and three more outhouses.

Only Dorothea was not assigned a job. She attended school with the other children. Maria became a typesetter in the print shop.

Everyone ate meals together in a large banquet hall. The walls were hung with beautiful tapestries. Chandeliers with lit candles hung from the vaulted wood ceiling. While everyone ate "together," in the same room at the same time, the men and the women ate at separate tables. There was no talking allowed. After prayers there was only the sound of eating. "I didn't know chewing sounded so loud," said Maria later. Her mother agreed.

Maria was not used to being served or not cleaning up after a meal. She no longer did any sewing, mending, or laundry. She no longer needed to embroider or paint for other people, and she had no classes to teach. She was not used to having extra time.

"Relax," her mother said.

"I don't know how," she replied.

When Maria wasn't needed in the print shop she explored the castle grounds. She discovered where the livestock were kept, the bakery, smithy, and the mill. She also met masons, carpenters, shoemakers, tailors, weavers, and bookbinders.

She and the girls visited Caspar often. With Caspar's help they quickly learned Dutch.

But...Maria was bored.

CHAPTER 18

What else could she do?

She looked through her notes and small paintings, the scattered items she used for reference when she made larger paintings. There was no organization to them. She had to hunt to find whatever she wanted. She took out sheets of paper, glue, pen and ink, and went to work.

First she glued three small paintings vertically on a page. Then she made a blue-gray paper frame around each painting. On the facing page she wrote about each small painting. Using her notes she copied where she had found the caterpillar and when, how it acted, what its food plant was. She wrote down how long it took to make its changes, and when it emerged as the butterfly or moth it became.

When Maria finished she bound all the pages

into a book. This book today is known as her Studienbuch, or Book of Studies.

After organizing her book of studies, Maria searched for something else to do. She found herself drawn to the kitchen gardens with all their herbs. She painted the chicory plant. They ate the young leaves in salads, the older leaves as a vegetable. A few days later she painted the red currant, used for making fruit soup, jam, and fillings for tarts. Marigolds came next. The fresh flowers were good crushed and rubbed on wasp or bee-stings. The dried flowers tasted good in a broth. And they were used to give cheese that yellow color.

Maria met many people while she lived with the Labadists. Among them were Jacob Herolt and Dr. Deventer. Both of them had been to South America, to the country of Dutch Guiana, also known as Suriname. While there both men had visited Governor Cornelius Sommelsdijk, brother to the sisters there at Castle Waltha. They also talked about a Labadist colony called Providencia, which was a large sugarcane plantation.

"Do the Labadists work in the fields of sugar cane?"

"Heavens, no! There are slaves to do that. It's much too hot for Europeans to work in those fields."

"Slaves?" asked Maria. "They have slaves?"

"Yes," replied Dr. Deventer. "They were brought from Africa specifically to work the sugar cane. All of the plantations rely on slaves."

Maria clamped her mouth shut, into a thin line.

Dr. Deventer continued talking, apparently

unaware of her reaction.

He talks about owning slaves as if that were perfectly acceptable, thought Maria. But she didn't voice her opinion. She continued listening to what they both had to say.

Dr. Deventer lived at Waltha Castle. He helped bring income to the group by making medical pills which were sold in the neighboring towns. He also had a library of medical books and nature books which he let Maria borrow.

In April 1686, while walking in the fields, Maria discovered frogs laying a lot of little eggs at one of the ponds. She watched them as closely as she did her caterpillars.

In her notes she wrote: "After a few days they showed signs of life and apparently ate from the white slime that surrounded them. Then tails appeared and they swam like fish. In the middle of May they had eyes, eight days later hind legs, eight days later front legs."

With four legs and a tail they looked like little crocodiles. Then they lost the tail and were able to go on land.

"Well, they certainly are not born through the mouth like a lot of writers said," she wrote.

Once again with her notes and paintings she proved the natural philosophers wrong.

CHAPTER 19

Things began to change.

Maria's beloved half-brother, Caspar Merian, died in April 1686. Now it was just the four of them—her mother, her two daughters, and herself. All contact with the other half-brothers and half-sisters had been dropped years ago. Maria busied herself even more with her herb paintings and searches for new caterpillars.

One day Johann showed up at Waltha Castle. "I have come to take you home," he said.

"I do not wish to go back to Nürnberg. This is my home, now."

"You are my wife. It is your duty to come."

"No, Johann. My life is here with the Labadists. You are not a member of this group, so we are no longer married."

Johann remained, hoping to convince Maria to

go back with him. He stayed in a visitor's house on the castle grounds. He did some manual labor for the community while he tried to convince Maria to return. He drew a map of the castle grounds showing all of the buildings, fields, and canals. He finally returned to Nürnberg alone.

Life at Waltha Castle continued as usual.

The Sommelsdijk sisters received another package from their brother in Suriname. He had sent more mounted butterflies for their collection, and the sisters invited Maria to see them.

"They are all so beautiful!"

Maria spent a long time looking carefully at each butterfly. She longed to see them alive, in their native habitat, instead of dead with a pin stuck through them.

Another change came in October 1688 which affected everyone at Waltha Castle. A letter arrived from Suriname. Governor Sommelsdijk was dead. He had been killed by a group of soldiers the previous July.

The murder of Cornelius Sommesldijk meant a large loss of income for the Labadist community. As the months passed, it became more and more difficult to take care of everyone. A few people left. More people talked about leaving. The rumble of discontent crept into the once peaceful community. More people left. The workload for those remaining became more difficult. There were rumors that the community might disband.

And then Maria's mother died.

Her mother's death hit harder than she expected. Growing up she had experienced the deaths of her three younger siblings, Max, Jacob, and Maria Elisabeth. The deaths of her stepfather and her half-brother were much more recent. But her mother had always been there. Now she was gone.

I will miss Mama, she thought. We didn't always agree, but she taught me how to run a household and how to embroider. She taught me well. Now there are just the girls and me. What should we do? Should we stay here? Where would we go?

CHAPTER 20

"Are we going to leave?" Dorothea asked her older sister, Johanna.

"Probably. We will have to ask Mama."

Their mother was at that moment discussing that very thing with the Sommelsdijk sisters.

"You can always return to Germany."

"No," said Maria. "There is nothing for me there."

Germany is even farther away from Suriname than Holland is, she thought.

"Maybe Amsterdam," she said. "I want to live where there will be the opportunity for a trip to South America someday. The port city of Amsterdam would be perfect."

"But you have no family to help you there."

"I have provided for myself and my family since my oldest daughter was born, and I have taken care of my mother since my stepfather died," said Maria. She raised her chin and sat up straighter. "I will once again provide for us just as I've done in the past."

The sisters looked at each other and nodded.

"Then we will contact the Witsens on your behalf. Dr. Nicolaas Witsen is Mayor of Amsterdam, and Jonas Witsen is the city secretary. They should be willing to help the well-known author of that famous caterpillar book."

Lucia smiled. "And they both have large collections of butterflies."

That evening Maria told her daughters they were leaving the castle.

"Where are we going?" asked Dorothea. "Is it far away?"

"We're going to live in Amsterdam," replied Maria. "It's not so far."

Johanna, Dorothea, and Maria packed their belongings. The girls helped their mother pack her art supplies, the copper plates, her study book, and of course, the boxes of caterpillars.

When the coach arrived they carried the boxes and bags out. Everyone said their goodbyes. Maria and the girls waved as the horses pulled the carriage down the lane, taking them away from this home.

"Are we going all the way by coach?" asked Johanna.

"Only part way. When we reach the coast we will go by ship the rest of the way."

At the quay Maria watched carefully, making sure their trunks and boxes were added to the correct group of luggage waiting to be hoisted up onto the ship. Satisfied, she and the girls joined the other passengers boarding the ship.

They found space at the rail and spent the next hour watching all the activity. Sounds surrounded them—the shouts of the ship's crew, the rumble of wagon wheels and the clop of horses' hooves on the cobblestones, dogs barking, seagulls swooping and crying overhead. People on the ship shouted conversations with people standing on the quay. And the ship creaked, gently rocked by the waves lapping against the hull. The slight movement of the ship was relaxing. Maria soon felt her worries slipping away, at least for now.

Finally everything was loaded and in place. The rest of the crew came on board and hauled in the gangplank. Some of the crew members climbed the rigging and went to work unlashing and spreading the sails. Others raised the anchor.

A gust of wind puffed out the sails. The ship creaked as it moved with the wind. Soon they watched the countryside slip by as the ship sailed south.

"Mama, we can see Amsterdam! Come look!" urged Dorothea.

"I will, Liebchen, as soon as I finish writing this note. I'll join you on deck"

"Hurry, Mama, It's Amsterdam!"

"Ja, ja, I'll be right there."

Maria dipped the quill pen she was holding into the open bottle of ink and finished writing. She set the pen down and closed the bottle. She removed the cork from a small bottle of sand and lightly sprinkled sand over the wet writing. The sand soaked up the excess ink so the writing would not smear. After a little bit it was safe to tilt the paper and let the sand slide off. She folded the paper from the edges inward. Next she lit a candle and sealed the note with a blob of melted wax. After that cooled she turned the folded paper over, and wrote "Nicolaas Witsen."

Then she went out to get her first look at Amsterdam.

It was a sunny day with a nice breeze. A group of white clouds passed quickly overhead, their shadows momentarily darkening the ship's deck and the water as they scudded across the sky.

The city stretched out across the horizon, brick and stone buildings four and five stories high. Tall towers and church steeples poked up into the skyline. Ships and boats were everywhere. Soon their ship dropped anchor and the crew hauled in and tied up the sails. They put down the gangplank and started unloading the luggage and other cargo. Passengers disembarked from other ships as well as their own, crowding the docks. Carriages and wagons arrived to pick up people and goods. It was a loud, noisy place, much louder than Harlingen where they boarded the ship.

Maria found a young boy eager to deliver her note to the mayor.

After a short wait a gentleman greeted them. "On behalf of Mayor Witsen, welcome to Amsterdam."

"Dank U weel," replied Maria. "Thank you very much."

"Come, I will take you to your new home in Vijelstraat, in the new part of the city."

They crossed three parallel canals that formed a half ring around the older part of the city. "These canals—the Herengracht, the Kaizersgracht, and the Prinsengracht—are where the wealthy merchants built their new houses," he said.

Vijelstraat crossed all three canals. This was a good location, near potential customers.

CHAPTER 21

After spending a few days settling in, Maria set out to visit Mayor Witsen. She knew instantly when she'd reached Dam Square. It was huge! And so was the Stadhuis (city hall).

The yellowish-white building stood five stories high. There was a domed cupola over the middle section. Instead of a fancy entrance there were seven plain arches at street level.

Inside she found herself in a large, brightly lit, very tall room. Sunshine streamed in through the high windows and made the crystal chandeliers sparkle against the columns and marble walls. She had to ask where the Mayor's office was.

"Welcome, Mevrouw Merian," said the mayor. "We are honored that you have chosen Amsterdam for your new home."

"Thank you, Mijnheer," she replied. "I came to

express my family's appreciation for your help in locating a place for us. It is in a lovely part of the city." They chatted for a few more minutes.

"You must visit the Medicus Hortus, our medicine garden," said the mayor. "We have herbs and other plants from all over the world in this garden. We are very proud of it."

"I look forward to seeing this Medicus Hortus very much."

"Please give my regards to Doktor Jan Commelin, the director of the gardens, when you visit."

Maria and her daughters walked east on Kerkstraat, on their way to the famous medical gardens. They would have to cross the Amstel River to get there.

"That's a skinny bridge!" said Dorothea when they reached the river. They crossed the narrow bridge, walking single file. Their full skirts brushed both sides of the bridge the entire length of it.

Once across the river they walked north where they soon reached the open gates of the medical gardens. Inside the big iron gates the noise of the busy city disappeared.

They wandered among the neat rows of plants and bushes. There were some plants they already knew. There were also many they had never seen before.

In the center of the gardens stood a long rectangular building. Johanna opened the door to this large building and they stepped inside. The scent of orange blossoms greeted them, along with heat and humidity. Maria soon wiped her face with the handkerchief she always carried.

Orange trees and palm trees in large pots pulled their attention up, away from the lower growing plants. They stared at the trees they had only seen before as drawings in books.

"Oh, my," said Johanna, her voice a mere whisper.

"They are something, aren't they, those trees?" said a gardener working nearby.

"They certainly are," said Maria. "No wonder Nicolaas Witsen suggested that I visit."

"The mayor told you to visit?" asked the gardner.

"Ja, he did. He is very proud of the Medicus Hortus."

"Indeed, we all are."

"He also asked me to give a message to Doktor Commelin. Do you know where I might find him?"

Footsteps sounded, getting louder as they came closer.

"I believe that's him now," said the gardener.

A distinguished looking gentleman came up and spoke to the gardener. "Some new plants have arrived and they need your attention," he said. The gardener nodded to him and to Maria and her daughters, and left. Doktor Commelin turned to also leave.

"A moment, Doktor Commelin," said Maria.

He stopped and looked at her, his eyebrows raised.

"Mijnheer Nicolaas Witsen asked me to give you his regards," she said.

"I don't believe we have met."

"No, we haven't," she agreed. "I am Maria Sybilla Merian, and these are my daughters, Johanna and Dorothea."

Instantly a smile appeared on Doktor Commelin's face and he stepped closer.

"Ah, the famous author of the caterpillar books." He gestured expansively. "Welcome to the Orangery. This is where we keep the plants that cannot survive the Dutch winters outside. Let me show you ladies around."

CHAPTER 22

Maria and her daughters left the Hortus Medicus gardens in high spirits. On the walk home they discussed their visit.

"I wonder if any butterfly eggs ever survived a voyage from the Indies?" Maria wondered. That would be something! But it would be even better to see them in their native habitat. Maria's longing to travel to South America became stronger.

The wealthy collectors and influential people of the city and the surrounding area quickly became a major part of Maria's life. They commissioned her to do paintings for them. Many had gardens of their own where she was allowed to come, search for caterpillars and draw from nature. But she did not limit herself to these private gardens. She also searched in the meadows and moors outside of the city. Once again the house quickly filled with boxes, baskets and jars of caterpillars and the necessary freshly picked leaves for each.

Maria needed more income, so she formed a new "Company of Maidens." She again taught daughters of the upper class how to embroider and how to paint with watercolors. She sold paint pigments ground and ready for use. She sold more of her first and second caterpillar books. If the buyer wanted colored illustrations then she and her daughters hand painted each page.

Soon Maria thought about publishing a third caterpillar book.

"We have found so many new caterpillars here in Holland, I'm sure we have enough for another book," she announced one evening.

"When will you have time to work on it?" asked Johanna.

Maria shrugged. "Oh, here and there, whenever I am not working on commissions."

Johanna grinned as she looked at her mother. "And when you are not visiting important people?"

"Or out searching the gardens and meadows?" added Dorothea.

"Or not teaching young ladies to embroider and paint," said Johanna.

"Or not..."

Maria threw her hands into the air. "Enough, enough! I'm only thinking about it right now."

Johanna and Dorothea looked at each other. They knew that one day they would be helping their mother get this book ready for publication.

CHAPTER 23

In July of 1692 twenty-four year old Johanna Helena Graff, Maria's oldest daughter, married Jacob Hendrik Herolt. If they followed the custom in Holland at the time, the door of the bride's house would have been painted green. Flowers would have been scattered around the door before the couple left for the city hall to be married in the required civil ceremony. At the celebration afterwards there would have been a special candy called "bridal sugar" and a spiced wine with floating bits of real gold called "bride's tears."

Maria's contacts continued to spread. One of those contacts was Agneta Block, a wealthy lady who owned a famous botanical garden at her country estate. Two of her prize acquisitions were a pineapple from Brazil, and a cactus from Curacao. Although she lived in Amsterdam she also spent time at her estate, which she called Vijverhof. The large white, two-story square house there faced the river and was easily reached by boat.

Johanna worked with her mother at this time, and both of them were invited to stay at Vijverhof and commissioned to create drawings of the some of the plants in the greenhouses.

By using her networking skills, Maria found yet another way to add to her income. Collectors continued to look for more unusual specimens to add to their collections. Maria wrote a letter to her friend, Clara Imhoff, in Nürnberg. She enclosed a small packet of carmine red pigment for painting. She also told Clara about the many rare specimens from the East and West Indies that she could get there in Holland. She then said, "...if anyone is a collector, I shall be happy to send some, if I could obtain in return all kinds of creatures found in Germany...." The creatures she specifically mentioned were snakes of all species, butterflies of all varieties, and stag beetles.

Maria continued, explaining how to put the snakes and similar creatures in jars filled with ordinary brandy, sealed with wood. Her instructions for preserving butterflies said that butterflies needed to be killed quickly. "One must hold the point of a darning needle in a flame," she wrote, "making it hot or glowing red, and stick it into the butterfly." That way the butterflies died immediately with no damage to their wings. She also wrote that "...the little boxes in which they are then placed can be coated with lavender oil first, so that no worms can get in and feed on them."

She finished her letter by adding that if anyone wanted to have any sort of seeds of Indian spices, they were also available in Amsterdam.

This new business of buying and selling imported items did bring her more income. But as she thought more and more about where the unusual items came from, she thought more and more about the beautiful butterflies of Suriname. She longed even more to travel to South America. Finally she made up her mind. She would go to Suriname.

Maria made a simple statement about her travel plans to a friend who stared at her in horror. "You cannot possibly do that! To Dutch Guiana? To Suriname? That kind of travel is much too difficult for women. The ocean trip alone is very dangerous––storms, pirates—much too dangerous for you!"

"Other people have survived," Maria said.

"It's a wilderness over there. The jungle is no place for women."

"I'd like to stay five years," Maria continued calmly.

"Five years? You are out of your mind!"

Everyone she knew made these same comments. Even Nicolaas Witsen was against her going. "You are already fifty years old," he pointed out.

"That is exactly why I must go," she said. "There is so much to learn. I've seen some of the butterfly specimens, but not the live butterflies. I have not seen the caterpillars they come from, nor what plants they eat."

"Who would go with you?" he asked.

"My daughter, Dorothea. She knows how to help with the research."

"But, Mevrouw Merian, women do not travel without a man. It's just not done!"

"I've done it before," she said, "when I moved to Castle Waltha with my mother and daughters, and again when my two girls and I moved here to Amsterdam."

"But to travel across the ocean? That's far more dangerous and difficult."

Maria refused to give up her dream.

During the following weeks she talked to Mijnheer Witsen again, and again mentioned Suriname.

"I could bring back new things for that nature cabinet," she reminded him, pointing to the cabinet where he kept his collection. His eyes betrayed his interest.

He was quiet for several minutes. Maria held back her excitement and kept quiet.

"Well...," he finally said, "three to five years is too long. I would advise two years at the most."

He told her everything he had learned from ship captains, businessmen, and letters from Providentia. Although the country was called Suriname by the people who lived there, he preferred to use the name which showed the Dutch ownership, Dutch Guiana. Then he calculated the amount of money it would take for Maria and her daughter to live in Dutch Guiana for two years. When he showed her the total, her eyes widened, her mouth opened but no words came out.

"So much!" she finally whispered. She would

have to sell all her household goods. Everything. She closed her mouth into a firm line, and nodded.

Nicolaas Witsen persuaded the city of Amsterdam to help fund Maria's trip.

Maria and Dorothea planned not only which clothes and personal items to take, but also how much parchment, paint pigments, brushes, and other things needed for their research. Maria also made a will.

The dream would soon be reality.

CHAPTER 24

Maria, now 52 years old, and Dorothea, 21, stood on the quay in the early evening and stared at the ship gently rocking in the water. It was Saturday, July 9, 1699. All passengers had to be on board before nightfall since they would leave Amsterdam early in the morning.

The ship, The Golden King, was a three-masted fluyt belonging to the WIC, the West India Shipping Company. It was a broad beamed, flat-bottomed ship 80 feet long. The hull curved back inward making the deck more narrow than the cargo bay. The bare masts and rigging shone in the evening sun. The crew used block and tackle to haul luggage and cargo aboard.

The sun inched its way to the horizon. Maria and Dorothea lifted their skirts slightly and walked up the sloped gangplank.

They watched other passengers arrive, all farmers by the looks of their clothing.

The light faded; time to go to their cabin. The gentle movement of the ship quickly lulled them both fast asleep.

Noises on deck woke Maria and Dorothea. The crew had raised the sails and tied them in place. Chains clanked and creaked as the anchor was hauled up. The ship slowly moved, and they had not yet left the cabin.

Maria and Dorothea stood at the deck rail watching the rays of sunshine slowly illuminate the city of Amsterdam. A few farmers joined them. A gust of wind caught the sails and the ship moved away from the dock. They watched the city fade into the distance.

"We are on our way at last," said Maria.

"Please, God, we're not attacked by pirates," grumbled one stodgy farmer.

"Pirates?" yelped Dorothea. She turned to her mother. "Pirates?"

"I believe I did hear about the possibility of pirates," said Maria calmly.

One of the farmers spoke up quickly. "They make surprise attacks on ships," he said. "They sail under a normal flag and then when they get close to you they change the flag to a skull and crossed bones."

"They don't need no gangplank to come aboard," said another. "They just climb right up the sides of the ship using an ax to help them."

"I heard they swarm over the side and show no mercy," said another. "And if they don't kill you right away, they take everything, including food, and leave you to die anyway."

Dorothea shivered.

"But not every ship is attacked. Pirates are not out there all the time," said Maria. "And remember, this ship is well armed against attacks."

Over the next few days Maria and Dorothea and the farmers talked a bit more. Slowly they developed a modest friendship, although the farmers mostly talked about the weather and crops.

July 14 was another lovely day. White clouds floated overhead as the ship sailed into the English Channel, into the Strait of Dover. "Look at those cliffs!" said Dorothea, pointing upward to the right. "They're so white!"

On July 16 there was no wind. The ship just sat there in the water. It wasn't going anywhere. The British coastline was not so interesting now.

Finally the wind picked up again and they sailed on to the Isle of Wight where the ship took on more cargo.

Two weeks later, the first of August, they reached the island of Madeira off the coast of Africa. The next day they saw Palma, in the Canary Islands, and by the ninth of August they were at Cape Verde, another island off the coast of Africa.

From Cape Verde they caught the trade winds which took them in a southwesterly direction, crossing the gigantic Atlantic Ocean towards Suriname. Maria and Dorothea spent many hours watching the continuously moving water, feeling the wind brush their faces. There was no coast to see, no islands. The clouds and the waves became their landscape, always changing, yet always the same.

The deck of the ship was rarely level. It was in constant motion dipping up or down from side to side, fore to aft. To their surprise they adjusted quickly to walking on this moving surface. The days became not only routine, but monotonous. The meals became monotonous, too. Every single morning started with a breakfast of groats (oatmeal). Other meals were mostly fish—salted or dried—and served with either peas or beans. There were no other vegetables. On Sundays they ate ham, lamb, or another salted meat. And beans. On Thursdays they had either beef or pork. And beans. The only fruit on board was dried apples. Bread? Only something called hardtack, a hard biscuit made of wheat and rye.

Dorothea and her mother were once again leaning on the rail staring into the distance. Dorothea turned and looked at her mother. Her shoulders slumped.

"It's been over a month now, and I'm tired of seeing just water, water, and more water."

Maria nodded. "I am tired of hardtack. I'm tired of...well most of all I'm tired of hardtack. I wonder if they have real bread in Suriname?"

They continued looking at the ocean and the empty horizon.

Another afternoon, when the ship's bell rang

eight times, Maria and Dorothea watched a member of the crew climb the rigging up to the crow's nest. It was a long way up there. They watched as he climbed over the protective railing and exchanged greetings with the sailor there. That sailor then scrambled over the railing onto the rigging and descended down to the deck.

He seemed to be a little wobbly at first when he stepped onto the deck and lurched sideways, closer to Dorothea.

"Are you all right?" she asked.

He nodded and ran his fingers through his hair. "I'll be all right now that I'm back down," he answered.

He noticed her puzzled look and explained. "The moving and swaying of the ship is much worse up there, and even the best seaman can get seasick up in the crow's nest."

"What's it like, being up there?" Dorothea asked. "Other than all that swaying?"

"Most of the time, once we're out on the ocean, it's rather boring. There's nothing to see but water. Sometimes it's difficult to pay attention. You don't want to get involved in your thoughts because then you could miss something. Like a pirate ship or a warship. Or a large floating tree trunk that could ram the ship."

"Does it ever get interesting?"

"Oh yes. I like to be up there on a clear morning and watch the sunrise. Sometimes porpoises swim alongside the ship. And I like to watch seagulls dive down into the water and come up with a fish in their beaks."

CHAPTER 25

On September 18, 1699, the ship reached the mouth of the Suriname River and began a slow turn, following the shoreline.

"We must be getting near," said Maria. "Look at all those boats."

"There's Fort Zeelandia," said one of the crew. He pointed to their right. "We'll be docking at Paramaribo soon."

"Finally. I will be so glad to be back on land."

The crew slowly, carefully brought the ship to shore and stopped alongside a huge rock sloping down to the quay. Chains clattered as the anchor lowered.

The harbor rang with noise from the ship and the dock. Men grunted as they moved boxes and crates. Periodically they stopped to wipe sweat off their faces. Seabirds wheeled overhead, calling loudly.

At last the gangplank was in place, sloping from the ship to the rock. Maria and Dorothea waved goodbye to the crew and disembarked. They stepped on shore...and found themselves unable to walk or stand straight. They lurched and reeled as if they were drunk.

"What's this?" asked Maria as she grabbed Dorothea's moving arm.

"You still have your sea legs," laughed someone nearby. "Don't worry, it will go away soon."

Clangs, bangs, and thunks followed the movement of cargo on shore. People shouted greetings and instructions.

"Bring that over here!"

"Make way!"

Clusters of people blocked their progress as they wobbled away from the ship. The hot sun beat down, the dry dust swirled only half-heartedly in all the commotion.

"Mevrouw Merian!" came a shout.

Maria and Dorothea both turned. A man, dressed in light colored clothing, with a wide brimmed hat on his head, pushed his way through a group of people, hurrying toward them.

"Goede dag," he said when he reached them. "Welcome to Paramaribo. I am a friend of Mijnheer Witsen. He asked me to meet you and take you to your new home. Come with me."

"How did you recognize us?" asked Dorothea. "You've never seen us before."

"Ah, that is easy. You are the only two women traveling without a man." He laughed.

"What about our things?"

"I have already seen to that. They will be delivered to your house later today. I trust you had a good voyage?"

"Ja," said Maria. "But it was a long one."

It took only a few minutes for them to reach the edge of town and the little wooden house, their home for the next two years. It looked very much like the houses in Holland, both inside and out. It was furnished, and they were delighted to find it stocked with basic food and supplies.

The following day Maria and Dorothea set out to explore Paramaribo. They were pleased to find that they could now walk without any problem. A row of trees on each side, mostly palms, shaded the wide dirt streets. The white wooden houses with dark green shutters were seldom more than two stories high. The hot sun beat down. The cooling breeze of the trade winds didn't help any in the direct sunlight.

On Waterkrant Street they found the busy, open air market. It looked nothing like the markets in Holland.

"What's that?" asked Dorothea, pointing to a funny looking, prickly thing with green spiky leaves coming out of the top.

"What's that?" asked her mother, pointing in a different direction.

"I wonder what these things taste like?"

"Are they cooked? Eaten raw?"

"There's a lot to learn, that's for sure," said Maria. She wiped her forehead with a handkerchief. Soon Dorothea did the same.

Maria wiped her face again and again. "It's so hot! Let's go back to the house. We can explore more later." They walked slowly in the heat, wiping beads of sweat from their faces.

The next few days were busy ones. Maria and Dorothea finished unpacking, and organized an area where they would keep the insects. They arranged a work area for painting and making notes. They explored the little town. And quickly learned to be outside early in the morning and to be back home during the hottest part of the day.

They made new friends and were soon introduced to one of the fruits of Suriname. They were served a dish with several yellow chunks of something that smelled wonderful.

"What is this?" asked Dorothea. "It smells lovely."

"It's a pineapple," answered their hostess. "It's one of my favorites. The minute one is cut this delicious smell fills the whole room."

Maria and Dorothea speared a chunk with their forks. Their eyes lit up, and they smiled as they savored the taste.

"Just remember," said their hostess, "that when you cut the outer part off, you must be sure to cut enough off. If you don't, there will still be little sharp hairs that will stick into your tongue when you try to eat it. And that hurts, really hurts."

"What does this pineapple look like before the outer part is cut off?" asked Maria.

Their hostess had an uncut pineapple brought in for them to see.

"It's that prickly thing we saw at the market!" exclaimed Dorothea.

Not only did they learn about new foods, they also had to learn the value of the different money used in Suriname. Some of the coins were the same Dutch coins they used in Amsterdam. But some were different. There were three small copper coins called Papagaaienmunt (parrot coins). The front of each of the three coins showed a parrot sitting on a tree branch. The branch had either one, two, or four leaves. The number of leaves showed the value of the coin...in sugar. One leaf meant the value was one pound of sugar. That meant one penny. Two leaves equaled two pounds of sugar, and four leaves equaled four pounds of sugar. Most astounding was that sugar was also used as money!

CHAPTER 26

"I wish we didn't have to wait for daylight. I'm ready to go now," said Dorothea.

Maria laughed. "I know. But just imagine trying to hold a candlestick and put caterpillars and leaves in the boxes at the same time. It would be difficult."

"Where shall we start looking?" asked Dorothea.

"I think we should start with the fields along the river and walk toward Fort Zeelandia. Later we can work our way around the city," said Maria.

The sun barely peeked over the horizon when Maria and Dorothea began searching for caterpillars along the river. The sun rose higher. The heat increased even though the trade winds breezed across their faces. They saw no caterpillars. It wasn't until they reached Fort Zeelandia that they found their first caterpillar.

Back in the welcoming shade of their house, they put the caterpillar and leaves into a larger box, wrote their notes and sketched the little creature.

It quickly became routine to search early in the day before it got so dreadfully hot. Soon their cottage was filled with caterpillars, other creatures, and some new noises, too.

One day they brought home some crabs and put them in a large clay pot with water. That night Maria and Dorothea were awakened by rustling sounds. They got up to investigate.

"Here's what's making that noise," said Dorothea. She held the candlestick above the clay pot. "It's the crabs moving around."

They discovered two creatures they did not like at all: mosquitoes and roaches. Although Dorothea and her mother wore long dresses with long sleeves, and slept under mosquito netting, some mosquitoes still managed to bite them. And those nasty roaches....

"I really hate them!" said Dorothea as another roach scurried under the pantry door. They found roaches everywhere and in everything, even their clothes. Roaches got into their food, especially anything sweet. And sometimes they found a roach in their drink!

On October 22, 1699, they searched in a small tree with tough, dark leaves, known as a guava tree. There they found a large, white caterpillar with black stripes around its body, and what looked like little red warts all along its sides. Maria plucked the "warty" caterpillar off the tree branch. Into the box it went, along with a supply of guava leaves and a small branch.

Soon the caterpillar spun a large grey cocoon on the branch. On January 22, three months after being taken off the guava tree, a white moth with many black stripes emerged.

Sometimes there were surprises.

Once they found a caterpillar covered with wriggly, white maggots. Ten days later the maggots turned into pretty, green flies. The caterpillar, of course, was dead.

In January, 1700, they searched farther out in a more isolated area. Among some very tall trees they spotted a yellow caterpillar with red stripes down the entire length of its body. It also had a dark brown head, and four quills sticking out of each body segment.

Back at the house where they could look at it more closely they made another discovery. Its feet were red. Within a short period of time the red-footed caterpillar turned into a chrysalis. Two weeks later they watched as the butterfly emerged and expanded its wings to dry. The wings were a radiant blue, green, and purple.

"Its shimmers like polished silver," said Maria. "There are no words to describe this beauty. I don't think brush and paint can capture how beautiful this butterfly is.

In February Maria and Dorothea searched through smaller trees known locally as Chinatrees. They found little green caterpillars with a yellow stripe over the whole body, and every segment had four yellow-orange spots with little hairs around each spot.

On February 18 they noticed that one of these unusual caterpillars had spun an ochre-colored cocoon. Almost a month later a large butterfly came out.

"Lieber Gott, that one can fly fast!" cried Maria. After they caught it they put it in a jar where they could better see it. Maria added to her notes: The spot on each wing looks as if it were a kind of glass.

Maria checked out the cocoons left behind by the emerging butterflies. "This looks like a strong thread they spun," she said. "I wonder if it would be a good silk?" She packed up a few of the empty cocoons and sent them back to Holland to find out.

CHAPTER 27

Maria looked up from the letter she held in her hands. "Dorothea, we are going to spend the month of April at Providentia."

"Is it nearby?"

"About forty miles downriver," said her mother. "A two day journey by boat."

The next message they received told them to be ready to leave in three days when the tide began rising. Also that their slaves would carry and load the bags and supplies.

Mid-morning three days later Maria and Dorothea walked to the dock on Waterkant Street. They were followed by three black slaves carrying their things. They were waved over to one of the wide, flat-bottomed wooden barges tied up at the quay. The slaves placed their loads in the middle of the barge, just in front of the seats in the back. The seats were covered by a flat roof resting on four posts. Because of this covered seating, built for plantation owners and their families, these boats were known as tentboats.

"Goede dag," said a man they assumed to be an overseer. He helped Maria and Dorothea into the boat and gestured towards the covered seats in the back. One black man untied the rope holding the boat, then joined the over seven already seated in front with long oars in their hands. They used the oars to push away from the shore, then rowed steadily down the river.

Everyone was quiet, focused on the rhythmic sound of the oars dipping into and lifting out of the water. They felt the oars' strong, steady pull through the water. On shore the buildings of Paramaribo gave way to fields, then trees, as far as they could see. Clouds in the sky created a moving patchwork of blue and white.

Farther on, the river narrowed and trees crowded the river.

"So many shades of green," said Maria. "Such a variety of shapes and sizes of leaves."

Nobody said anything for a while. Then Maria leaned towards the riverbank.

"Look," she said, pointing. "Over there. It looks like eyes in those two little brown bumps sticking out of the water."

"Crocodile," said their guide.

The croc moved slightly and they saw the length of its head. Small ripples in the water bobbed gently away as it floated just beneath the water's surface.

"Is it dangerous?"

"You best stay away from them. They're usually along the riverbanks or in the water."

Maria nodded.

In late afternoon, at a sharp bend in the river, the slaves turned the boat and rowed to a wooden dock. The dock looked just like the others they had seen along the way. One slave tied up the boat as another jumped onto the dock and rang a bell attached to the top of a post.

"We will stay here until the tide turns again."

"Are they expecting us?"

"No. But every plantation owner is prepared for visitors because no one can continue traveling at low tide or after dark. We will leave in the morning."

Slaves from the plantation came to help carry the luggage. Maria and Dorothea followed the overseer up the path away from the dock.

The white wooden manor house stood two stories high. It had tall windows and an open porch designed to catch the breezes.

"Goede avond," said the plantation owner. "Welcome to our home."

"Thank you," replied the visitors.

"Kwasiba, show the women to their room at the head of the stairs."

The slave bobbed her head and motioned for Maria and Dorothea to follow her.

Later as they walked down the wide stairs, they heard voices from the porch.

"She's doing what?"

"Like I said, she's coming to Providencia to

collect caterpillars. Her daughter helps her."

"Why would anyone travel all the way to this country just to do that? There are plenty of caterpillars in the Netherlands."

"Ja, there are many caterpillars in the Netherlands," said Maria as she stepped onto the porch. "But the ones here are not like the ones there. I have seen collections of butterflies from Suriname, and I want to know what kind of caterpillar they were before they transformed into butterflies."

The plantation owner cleared his throat. He gave a quick, dismissive wave of his hand.

"Everybody comes here for the sugar, that's what is important. Sugar is our life. Nothing else matters."

Maria smiled and shook her head. They would never understand.

Early the next morning very loud, deep guttural growls and bellows startled Maria and Dorothea awake. They sat up in bed, eyes wide, shivers racing up and down their backs.

They got out of bed and ran to the window.

"Can you see anything?"

"No, it's still too dark." They stared out the window trying to see if anything moved outside. The howling and growls continued, but did not get any closer.

Daylight slowly crept through the windows.

"We heard the most awful noise this morning just before sunrise," said Maria at breakfast.

"That must have been the howler monkeys," said their host. "We are so used to them that we don't pay any attention anymore. They are little monkeys with huge voices that live in the treetops. They won't come near, you don't have to worry about them."

After breakfast they continued their journey. In the middle of the afternoon, the slaves turned the tentboat towards another wooden dock at the edge of the water.

CHAPTER 28

"Welcome to Providencia."

Maria and Dorothea were greeted warmly, if also a little curiously, by the Labadists.

A young slave girl led the way to their room. Two more slaves brought in their luggage, boxes, and art supplies. Dorothea and her mother unpacked,

They joined the others in the dining salon when it was time to eat. After the evening meal Maria and Dorothea sat on the porch with their hosts where they could enjoy the evening breeze.

"How many members live here?" asked Maria.

"There are now only thirty. That's not counting the slaves, of course. Some of our people became tired of the plantation life and left. They went either to Paramaribo or back to Holland," answered the lady sitting next to Maria.

"And you, do you and your daughter really spend your days chasing after caterpillars, and bring them back to your house?"

Maria nodded. "We do." She smiled. "These small insects are such good examples of God's handiwork. And the transformation they go through to become butterflies and moths is amazing!"

Soon everyone sitting on the porch joined in a lively discussion, mostly asking Maria and Dorothea questions about their work.

Darkness crept over the landscape. A few people left the porch and went inside. Conversation slowed, then stopped.

"What are all the buildings?" asked Dorothea.

"Living quarters, mostly," replied the woman sitting to her right. "The long one-story buildings with thatched roofs are for the slaves. The smaller buildings near those are the kitchens and storage buildings."

"Why is the kitchen not with the house?"

"One reason is the danger of fire. Another is that the cooking fires make the kitchen very, very hot. Having it separate from the house keeps the house from getting that hot as well."

"It must be terrible for the cooks, then."

"That's why cooking is a job for the slaves."

Loud howling woke Maria and Dorothea again early the next morning. This time they knew what it was, but even so they could not go back to sleep. They dressed, gathered boxes, supplies, and left the house. They looked for caterpillars, checking for holes in leaves and chewed leaf edges. They turned leaves over to see if any tiny eggs were stuck to the underside.

They checked out nearby plum trees. They found some prickly, green caterpillars. But the caterpillars were not eating the leaves of the tree, they were eating the flowers. Only when the blossoms were gone did the caterpillars eat any leaves.

On April 5 Maria noticed that the plum tree caterpillars were not moving. Two days later they changed into their chrysalis form.

Maria and Dorothea were very busy in Providencia. Every day they collected and collected and collected. They brought back to the house plants, bugs, birds, butterflies, caterpillars and their food plants. They wrote many notes and made many sketches.

A lot of rubber trees grew wild on the plantation. Among those trees they found a large black and green striped caterpillar. At the end of the month the caterpillar enclosed itself into a round, wood-colored form.

One evening Maria and Dorothea decided to watch the sun come up. So, early the next morning, at 3 a.m., they got up, dressed, and ventured out into the moonlight. Everything was very still.

"Trees and bushes that stand around the house are asleep," wrote Maria. "The leaves are folded together. Most of the flowers are closed."

They stood under a tall mango tree. The thick foliage protected them from the morning dew.

"The fresh morning breeze stirs from time to

time billowing the sweet perfume of flowers to us. Large moths flutter like ghostly shadows in the moonlight around us," she wrote.

Eventually the sky turned a soft grayish red. The outlines of trees became more distinct. Tree branches and leaves moved in the wind.

"The forest awakes. Nature bathes in the fresh air of the morning. Bugs fly, birds call, gnats buzz. And though we cannot see them, in the thick tree tops just awakened monkeys quarrel and scream." Maria and Dorothea were now accustomed to the sounds the little monkeys made. The loud, deep noises almost like the growl of a large beast no longer scared them.

Damp, a little stiff from the cool air, tired and hungry, Maria and Dorothea hurried back to the house.

After breakfast they gathered their painting supplies, chairs and umbrellas. They left the house to work outside. They carried some of the things themselves. The rest was carried by the slaves assigned to go with them into the jungle. Once they reached the place they had decided on, they set up, began drawing, and carried on a lively conversation with their slave companions.

Maria enjoyed talking with people, even when she disagreed with them. The merchants and slave owners could not understand her interest in caterpillars and nature. She could not understand their lack of interest in anything except sugar. The wretched treatment of slaves upset her. The plantation owners believed that slaves were less than human. She learned that many slaves escaped from their owners. And when those escaped slaves were caught they were treated very badly.

"Oh yes, when we catch a runaway slave we cut the Achilles tendon completely through," commented one slave owner.

"But that tendon joins the calf muscle to the heel," said Maria. "That means the person's foot cannot function. Surely he cannot work very well then. If he can't work, why would you do that?"

"As an example to all the other slaves," snorted the owner. "Everybody knows that. And if another one escapes, when we catch him, we amputate his right leg." He slapped his knee for emphasis.

Maria's friendliness towards the slaves and Indians irritated the whites. But the slaves and Indians helped her in her research. She developed a good relationship with the people so easily dismissed by the colonials.

Soon came the time to pack for the return trip to Paramaribo. They now had many boxes and baskets full of caterpillars and other specimens to take with them. When everything was loaded onto the tent boat, Maria and Dorothea stepped into the boat, sat down under the wooden canopy, and waved goodbye. The slaves pushed the boat away from the dock and began paddling upstream.

CHAPTER 29

Back in Paramaribo their research continued. One May morning they searched through some large grape leaves. Dorothea reached for a green caterpillar. It had four white wavy spots on its sides with a green spot in the center of each white spot.

"Ach!" she cried, jerking her hand back.

Foam ran from the caterpillar's mouth. "When I touched it," said Dorothea, "it made itself shorter and did that."

They took it home. In the middle of May it shed its skin and became a brown chrysalis. On June 6, a gray owl butterfly with brown flecks and white stripes emerged. Its feet were white, and the mouth a golden yellow.

On June 3 Maria noticed that one of the round, wooden-colored cocoons they had brought back from Providentia was moving. Dorothea joined her and together they watched a butterfly with curvy brown and white stripes come out and spread its wings.

In July they found a caterpillar with a square body. Both ends were blue, the middle was green. Dorothea picked it up.

"Oh," she said, "its feet are sticky."

"There should be something really unusual come from this one," Maria said. They were disappointed when it turned out to be not very pretty.

They had better luck with a caterpillar they found on a grapefruit tree. The caterpillar was green with a blueish head. The body had long, prickly spikes almost as hard as wire. On August 19 it became a butterfly that shimmered with black, green, dark blue, and white in the light.

"That's the butterfly that is so fast and flies up so high," said Maria.

Not all of the caterpillars became moths or butterflies. They found one yellow caterpillar with a little black head and rows of short black bristles down its back.

"It reminds me of a clothes brush," said Maria.

That "clothes brush" caterpillar became a large, black bee with yellow rings around its body.

Another caterpillar became one of those pesky wasps that were everywhere.

Once they brought home some white worms they found on a plant. They put them all in a wooden box. When they later checked, the worms were gone. There was now a hole in the box. The caterpillars had chewed through and crawled away.

One day Maria saw a wasp's nest in front of her window. She was curious so she brought it inside. Every day she watched the wasps drag small caterpillars into the nest. Finally she had seen enough. She tore the nest apart, and chased the wasps out!

CHAPTER 30

Evening shadows stretched longer as the sun sank lower.

Someone knocked on the door. Maria opened it and there stood a few of their Indian friends. One of them handed her a cloth sack. "Lantern Carriers," he said. Then they turned and disappeared into the evening shadows.

Lantern Carriers! She had heard about them but had not found any. What a great gift. It was late, though, so they would look at them in the morning. She put the untied sack in a box with a lid.

Night slipped into the bedroom. One by one the lights in Paramaribo went out.

Mother and daughter slept.

A noise, a loud continuous thrumming noise

filled the house. Maria and Dorothea jerked awake, sitting up in bed, wide-eyed.

"Lieber Gott!" whispered Maria. "What is that?"

Dorothea's hand shook as she lit the candle. She got out of bed and picked up the candlestick. Her mother joined her, and walking very close together, they headed for the bedroom door. Maria reached for the door handle, hesitated, then slowly opened the door.

The noise increased as the door opened, and got louder and louder as they slowly followed the sound. It led them to the wooden box that held the Lantern Carriers. Maria picked up the box. It vibrated. She looked at Dorothea who looked at the box.

"Should we open it?" Her voice shook.

"I think I must," said her mother. "Otherwise we will never know for sure...."

She lifted the lid. Blaring noise and bright lights came flying toward her face. She screamed and dropped the box. Dorothea screamed, too. Lights spun all around the room.

Late the next morning they stared at the box for a long time. It did not move. It was very quiet.

"Shall we open it now?" asked Dorothea.

Maria yawned. "Be careful. I don't want to spend another hour chasing them again."

Dorothea slowly raised the lid. The Lantern Carriers sat quietly in the box. She reached in, picked up one, and closed the lid. She opened her hand. The bug barely moved on her flattened palm.

They gazed at the three-inch long bug with its

wings folded at its sides. It looked like a cicada, except for that peanut shape in front of its head. The eyes were tiny, not like a cicada.

"The peanut shape looks translucent, even with those brown shapes and lines on it. That must be what lights up."

"It's hard to believe they can make that much light."

"Ja," agreed Maria. "You could probably read a newspaper by the light they made."

Dorothea put the Lantern Carrier back in the box with the others. They barely moved. "I can't believe these are the same bugs we chased last night," she said.

Maria and Dorothea continued collecting insects, studying them and writing notes. They painted illustrations of what they saw. Flying insects often pestered them as they worked, especially bees and wasps.

"It's either the color, or something in the paint," said Dorothea. "Shoo! Go away!"

And then there were those pesky mosquitos. They were often a nuisance, their bites itchy. The bite of one of those tiny mosquitos would soon disrupt Maria's plans.

CHAPTER 31

Outside one morning, while searching for caterpillars, Maria began rubbing her arms. A few minutes later she was visibly shaking.

"Mama, what's wrong?" asked Dorothea.

"I'm a little chilly," said her mother.

"Chilly? In this heat?"

"Ja, it is so."

Dorothea stared at her mother. "We go back to the house, NOW!"

Dorothea bundled her mother in whatever she could find to add warmth. Maria still shivered uncontrollably.

An hour or so later she suddenly threw all of it off.

"Now I'm hot," she complained. A fever and headache settled in. Then came the nausea and vomiting. Her legs ached. Her fingers ached. She ached all over.

She started sweating again. It seemed like it would never quit. Soon she and the bed were drenched. Dorothea changed the bed linens and helped her mother change clothes. Much later her mother fell into an exhausted sleep. Maria had malaria, one of the most dangerous diseases on the planet.

Nobody knew what caused this sickness. It seemed to be connected with swampy, wet places. They decided that the swamps contaminated the air that people breathed. So the disease was named mal'aria, meaning bad air.

The next day Maria felt somewhat better, but very tired. Within the hour, though, she began shivering. Oh, no, not again.

The cycle continued every few days. Each time was less severe than the last. More and more days passed between attacks. Then they stopped.

Maria knew that she must leave South America. This illness could return, and she might not survive next time. With mixed feelings she and Dorothea began to plan their return to Amsterdam.

Rumors of war reached Paramaribo by the end of May, 1701. Charles II of Spain had died. He had no children. The next in line to his throne was a relative in France. If Spain and France worked together, it would upset the balance of power in Europe. It could also have an effect in Suriname because Spain owned a lot of land in the Americas. The armies of Spain, France, England, and the Netherlands were ready for battles at sea.

It was more important than ever for Maria and Dorothea to leave Suriname—as soon as possible. Their research stopped immediately. Maria booked passage for their return trip. They began the long task of packing everything to be shipped. On June 11, 1701 Maria closed and packed her notebook.

Once again they stood in the heat on the crowded, busy, noisy dock. They said their final farewells to friends who had come to see them off, then joined the other passengers boarding the ship De Vreede (the Peace). The crew aboard the ship and the men working on the dock carefully winched all the passengers' baggage onto the ship and stowed it all below deck. The ship was due to sail in the morning.

That night Maria and Dorothea slept in their cabin on the ship. In the morning they awoke to loud yelling and screaming. They dressed quickly and went on deck. The passengers bellowed and shouted. The crew tried to calm the angry passengers, but raised their voices even louder trying to be heard.

Maria looked around. Her eyes widened. Trees stood quite close to the ship. There had been no trees near the ship last night. Several people jabbed their fingers, pointing across the river. Paramaribo and Fort Zeelandia were on the other side! How did that happen? More importantly, would they still be able to sail that day?

It turned out to be a huge delay. Cap was not on board. The First Mate sh ordered the ship to be moved into deeper wate shore for the night. Instead he went to sleep. The ship stayed in the shallow part of the river where it had been for loading. During the night, at high tide, the ship slipped its anchor. The moving water easily took the ship across the river where it ran aground.

Several days went by. As it was the rainy season, a downpour of rain often forced the passengers into their small cabins. Nobody knew when they would be able to leave.

The news was not good. The Governor would not let the ship sail until it was decided who should pay for the damage. The First Mate said it should be the Captain, the Captain said it should be the First Mate.

Three weeks later on July 5th they still had not sailed. Everyone on board worried.

Finally the matter was settled and they sailed north into the Caribbean. There they caught the easterly winds that would take them back across the Atlantic Ocean.

Each day ran into the next with a boring sameness. Except for the day the caiman hatched. (What everyone had called crocodiles were actually the smaller caiman.)

That day started out like all the others. Maria and Dorothea had been on deck most of the morning. They went back to the cabin to check on the chrysalises, to see if there was any change.

They heard something. They lifted the lid off a crate. Inside sat a smaller box where Maria had carefully packed three caiman eggs.

"Uh, uh, uh."

One of the eggs moved slightly. It cracked. "Uh, uh, uh, uh."

They waited. A head popped up out of the egg. It stayed like that, apparently resting. Then, in the blink of an eye the entire caiman was out of the egg, looking around.

It was about 8 or 9 inches long, with a short snout. The body was yellow with black spots and bands. Its yellow eyes had a vertical black strip of color.

The caiman climbed over the edge of the box and dashed over the other contents of the crate.

Dorothea quickly removed some of the crate's contents so the caiman could not escape. They put some of their water in a small dish. The caiman immediately climbed into the dish. A minute later it was out running around, again trying to climb the sides of the crate.

On the third day the caiman was no longer so active. There was no food to be had. It needed more un-salty water, also not available. Its skin was already drying out. There was nothing they could do.

On the fourth day the caiman died.

Dorothea and Maria found the brandy and extra jars they had packed in the crate. They poured brandy into one of the jars and placed the little caiman in the brandy to preserve it. After they arrived in Amsterdam the caiman would be sold to a collector as a specimen for his curiosity cabinet.

The rest of the voyage became routine again, checking the chrysalises, strolling on deck, and conversations with other people on board the ship.

CHAPTER 32

Friday, September 23, 1701. The ship docked in the Amsterdam harbor. Chains clanked as the heavy anchor descended in the water. Maria and Dorothea stood at the rail with the other passengers, eagerly waiting until they could leave the ship. They watched the activity, listened to the voices, the sound of the horses' hooves and the creak of wagons and carriages.

Maria inhaled the crisp autumn air. This was quite different from their arrival in South America, Maria thought as she remembered the oppressive heat that had greeted them in Paramaribo.

Maria and Dorothea moved into a house on Spiegelstraat, close to where they had lived before.

As in all the houses, there was only a narrow staircase going upstairs. It was not wide enough for anyone to carry up large boxes, trunks, or furniture. However, there was the arm of a lever mounted on the gable of the house. A set of pulleys was added and soon all the boxes and trunks were hoisted up and pulled in through a window. The fronts of the houses were tilted toward the street so that the houses themselves did not get scraped in this process.

Maria was invited to display some of her collections from Suriname in City Hall. The display was a sensation. Most of it—including the caiman and a hummingbird—was totally new to the Europeans, and they were as excited as Maria and Dorothea had been.

Maria was asked so often if she was publishing a book about their stay in Suriname she began thinking about it. She looked through her notes, drawings and paintings. She set aside what she might use. She totaled up the amount of money she would need.

"Ach, meine Gute!" she cried. "The cost, it is so much!"

Still, she continued thinking about the book. It must be a magnificent book, not like anything done before. She would show all the moths, butterflies, and other creatures life size. That meant using a full folio sheet for each page instead of the one-fourth size like she'd used before. Four times the cost for paper alone.

"That's a lot of money," she kept saying. "I don't

know...."

"That has not stopped you before," said Dorothea. She reminded her mother that she had always set goals, and managed to achieve them. Even when other people were sure she could not. "This book will be no different."

"You are right," said Maria. "I will do this. Now, how can I raise the amount of money I need? I have specimens we brought back to sell to collectors. What else can I do?" She stared into the distance.

But before all of those decisions were made, there was a wedding to consider.

Dorothea Graff, age twenty-three, married Philipp Hendriks of Heidelberg. The civil ceremony was performed by the Registrar of Marriages at City Hall. Philipp moved into their house since, as a ship's doctor, he was often gone—sometimes a year at a time. Dorothea continued working with her mother.

Maria sat at the window and stared out somewhere between the red tile rooftops and the puffy clouds drifting across the sky. She was so lost in her thoughts that she was unaware of the activity on the street below. She didn't even hear the clatter of the cart wheels as they bumped across the cobblestones. Even the odor of freshly dropped road apples did not bother her.

What to include in this new book? The big blue butterfly, for sure. That yellow caterpillar that looks like a clothes brush. So many unusual caterpillars to choose from.

She began her book with the pineapple and the

insects she found on them. On the first page she showed the plant blooming. On the next page she painted the ripe fruit. She also included the Kakerlaken (roaches) because they laid their eggs on the pineapple plant. She wrinkled her nose and frowned. Kakerlaken! They invaded every house, got into clothes, food and drinks, spoiling everything. Nasty little creatures!

It felt good to be working on a book again.

In the following weeks Maria referred often to her notes, small paintings, and the preserved specimens they had brought back.

"You are painting more than just caterpillars this time, aren't you," said Dorothea.

Maria nodded. "I simply cannot leave out those other unusual creatures. Remember those big black, hairy spiders with the sharp teeth? One page is just for them and those very large ants."

The ants that nothing stopped. The ants that created a bridge of themselves when necessary for other ants to use. The ants that came out of the forest and into everybody's houses once a year. They ate just about everything in the house, then marched together to the next house, and then the next. Only after they finished with the last house did they go back into the forest.

Maria accepted a commission to paint illustrations for a book by someone else. It was called D'Amboinsche Rariterkamer (Curiosity Cabinet of Amboina), written by Georg Eberhard Rumphuis. He lived on an island in the Ambon archipelago. He collected the plants, hard and soft shellfish, rocks, minerals, and fossils of Ambon. Then he wrote about them and drew them all. He shipped his work to the Dutch East India Company in Amsterdam. It never arrived.

His original manuscript and drawings were lost at sea when the ship it was on was attacked and sunk. Now blind, he was unable to recreate the artwork. Maria had to work from his descriptions.

"I am sure some, maybe all, of these things can be found in the collections here," said Maria. "I shall have to match the descriptions with what I see in those collections." She began painting illustrations of the shells that Rumphius described. The page was filled with shells, each one carefully separated from the rest. This method of illustration was very different from those she made for her own books. It also kept her from working full time on her own book. But she needed the money.

"I was just looking through our notes," said Dorothea. "Remember these brown and white spotted caterpillars?" She held the open book towards her mother.

"Ja, I remember. When I disturbed them, they stuck out yellow feelers on their heads." She smiled. "I guess they were trying to decide if we were friendly or not."

A small painting of a yellow caterpillar with red tufts and a red head drew their attention.

"We found two of them, but one died. The one that survived became a beautiful large blue butterfly with lacy patterns on the edges of its wings." It would be included in the book.

Maria received many letters from friends. She often wished she had wings so she could fly to see them. "These days I feel like the frying pan on feast days, I have so much to do. I must put off writing to them for awhile longer."

The "frying pan on feast days" that she talked about was the tradition of eating pancakes—many pancakes—on the Tuesday before Lent (the forty days before Easter). No dairy products could be eaten during that time. To keep those items they already had from spoiling, the women made a lot of pancakes to use up their supplies of fat, butter, and eggs.

Maria wrote many business letters to sell her specimens to collectors in Amsterdam and other places. In October, 1702, she wrote to Johann Volkamer in Nürnberg to tell him what she still had. She mentioned one caiman, various snakes and other creatures in jars of brandy. She also had twenty boxes of butterflies, beetles, hummingbirds, and lantern carriers. "The lantern carriers," she wrote, "produce such a loud noise that you want them away from you." She then wrote a little about her trip, signed the letter and left it on the table so the ink could dry.

CHAPTER 33

Maria placed a package on her work table. She carefully unknotted the string and removed the brown paper wrapping. She placed one of the gleaming sheets of copper on the table. The rest she carefully put away. She chose a painting from those she done, and placed it beside the sheet of copper, gathered her engraving tools and sat down.

A short time later she put down the engraving tool. She closed her eyes and massaged her forehead. "I cannot do any more of the engravings for my book. It will be all I can do to finish this one. I just don't have the strength." She sighed.

Maria hired three of Holland's best engravers. Pieter Sluyter engraved 35 plates, Joseph Mulder engraved 21 plates, and Daniel Stoopendael who engraved just one.

Meanwhile, Maria went back to painting another illustration. This time it was a cashew tree with the fruits called cashew apples. She added a red caterpillar with black bands around its body crawling from one of the apples onto the stem. The kidney-shaped cashew nut hung from the bottom of the apple.

Maria wrote how the Indians ate baked cashew nuts to stop diarrhea, and to get rid of worms. She told how the colonists were not willing to use things available in Suriname. She did not understand why they ignored what grew there just because it was different, and instead imported all the things they were used to.

In another illustration for the new book, Maria painted a green caterpillar among the small white flowers of the Spanish plum tree. On a branch below the flowers she painted a cluster of plums. "The Europeans ignore this local source of fruit, preferring to plant only sugar cane," she wrote.

Promoting interest in her book was next. She needed a good plan. Showing and writing about all the rare and unusual insects, plants, and animals of Suriname was not enough. Her expenses were mounting and the book was not yet ready for the printers. She still needed money.

Once again Maria came up with a creative solution: a subscription. If you ordered a copy of the book before it was published, you paid less. Everybody liked to get something for less. She sat at her desk with paper, uncapped the bottle of ink, and reached for her quill pen. She wrote to all the collectors she knew and told them about the subscription.

On June 4, 1703, Maria sent a letter to James Petiver in London. Mr. Petiver was interested in her new book; he was also a Fellow in the Royal Society in London. This was a group of men promoting knowledge of nature by observing it and by experimenting. Maria sent a sample print from her new book, and information about the subscription. She also asked him to promote her book among his friends.

On June 20, she wrote to Mr. Petiver again, saying that she would like to have her book announced in an English newspaper. She asked him if he would do that.

A letter arrived from Mr. Petiver. Maria broke the wax seal and unfolded the paper.

"It's a copy of the advertisement," she said with a smile. "Let's see what he wrote."

He mentioned her already published two books about the insects of Germany and Holland. And that she had recently returned from Suriname. There was Maria's proposal to publish a book "...about the transformations of the caterpillars in Suriname observed and illustrated by Maria Sybilla Merian." He included the subscription and the rate of thirty shillings payable in three installments. The last line of the advertisement read, "The work is highly approved of by all that see it."

"I hope there are a lot of subscribers now," said Maria, "especially since it was published in the journal of the Royal Society of London."

The last illustration was finished. Maria now wrote the descriptions for each of the sixty illustrations. She included extra information about some of the plants, fruits, and customs of Suriname. Caspar Commelin, from the Medicus Hortus, added some botanical information about the plants.

Maria continued promoting her book, but she closed the discounted subscriptions. People who ordered the book now had to pay full price.

"Mama, the books are ready!" said Dorothea. She handed her mother a large, mottled, leather bound book.

Maria held the book. She ran her fingers across the impressed, gold leaf panel design on the front cover. She opened the book and read the title page. Metamorphosis Insectorum Surinamensium. The Metamorphosis of Insects of Suriname. She had done it! She hugged the book to her chest.

Maria remembered when she had not been taken seriously, when many people would not pay attention to what she had to say because she was "a mere female." She remembered when her interest in caterpillars had been thought strange, when she herself had been thought strange. Like all women she had been denied attendance at any university and membership in any scholarly organization. A nobody. Now she was both well-known and a respected authority on metamorphosis!

EPILOGUE

Maria Sybilla Merian died in 1717. Many of her works, including her Studienbuch, her book of studies, were bought by Tzar Peter (the Great) of Russia. It is said that he purchased these on January 13, the same day she died. He built a museum in St. Petersburg to showcase her work and other collections.

Maria had already finished most of the illustrations for a third caterpillar book. Shortly after her death, Dorothea completed the remaining ones. She also published the book, completing the set of three books showing the life cycles of Europe's caterpillars and butterflies.

Maria Sybilla Merian is known today as a woman who persevered, a woman who did not let obstacles keep her from doing what she felt was important—something both scientifically informative and artistically beautiful. And today she is known as the Mother of Entomology.

ABOUT THE AUTHOR

Nancy Dailey
(Photo by Bob Linder}

After graduating high school Nancy Dailey spent a year in Germany where she learned the language. She continued studying art and German in college, and obtained her degree from the University of Missouri. She also studied writing with the Institute of Children's Literature.

She exhibited her artwork in regional, national, and international shows for several years before concentrating her time and energy on teaching in the public schools of Missouri. She developed several innovative programs which she used in her classroom. Nancy has published in area newspapers and in local, regional and national magazines, as well as online.

With more than 30 years in a classroom, she decided to make a change. At the age of 70, Nancy Dailey chose to go zip-lining through the trees and has been going non-stop ever since. Her two daughters encourage her in all of her varied interests, including geocaching, zip-lining, hunting for treasure, seashells, and new hobbies. When she's not traveling, she's painting, writing, or otherwise being creative.

ABOUT THE TIME PERIOD

Other bits about the time in which Maria Sybilla lived.

Early "scientific" observations were not always accurate. Many people still believed in spontaneous generation—that living things could come from non-living things. Because of this they often jumped to conclusions. An example is the following work of a Dutch doctor.

In 1620 Dr. Jan Baptista van Delmont wrote and published a paper to prove that living things *did* come from non-living things. Based on what he had seen, he wrote a recipe for making mice! According to Dr. van Delmont, if you put a piece of sweaty, smelly underwear in an open mouth jar and added some grain, in twenty-one days full-grown mice would emerge.

Before streets had names, how could one find a shop or where someone lived?

Well, in Nürnberg there were statues placed on the corner of one of the buildings at a street intersection. These were used as reference points to help guide you to the correct place

A once-in-a-lifetime event took place in Frankfurt on August 1, 1658, when Maria was eleven years old. Leopold, the new Holy Roman Emperor, was crowned in the *Dom*—a church called a cathedral even though it wasn't. Afterwards the royal procession paraded from the church to the city banquet hall a few blocks away. Fancy dressed courtiers, counselors, knights, and drummers led the procession. The new emperor walked under a canopy held above his head. Other officials followed. Treasury clerks came last on horseback, throwing newly minted coins into the crowd.

After the emperor had been served in the banquet hall, a huge public feast began outside, where the celebrating lasted until the sun went down.

These are some of the coins Maria could have used.

Nürnberg 1678
1 Kreuzer

Frankfurt 1647
1 Albus

Netherlands 1690
6 Stuivers

Suriname 1679
Parrot coin equaled 2 pounds of sugar. One pound of sugar was worth 1 cent.

This is a Lantern Carrier like the one that scared
Maria and Dorothea.
The wingspan is over three inches.

Here you can see the peanut shaped head.

(Photos by Mamoru Seki)

A Blue Morpho butterfly caught (and released) in
the rainforest of Suriname.

(Photo by Felix Sanders)

148

SOURCES

BOOKS:

Chrysalis, Maria Sibylla Merian and the Secrets of Metamorphosis by Kim Todd
Harcourt, Inc. 2007

The Cost of Sugar by Cynthia McLeod
Hope Road Publishing, London 2011 (e-book)

Ein Schmetterling aus Surinam by Ingrid Möller
Beltz & Gelberg 1995

Eine Frau, drei Männer und eine Kunstfigur, Barocke Lebensläufe by Wilhelm Treue
Verlag C. H. Beck, München 1992

Eyewitness Travel Amsterdam
Dorling Kindersley 2007

Frankfurt Through the Centuries by George G. Wynne
Waldemar Kramer, Frankfurt 1957

Insects of Suriname, Metamorphosis Insectorum Surinamensium 1705
by Maria Sibylla Merian, Introduction by
Katharina Schmidt - Loske
(reprint based on copy owned by Öffentliche
Bibliothek, Universität Basel)

Metro Books by arrangement with Taschen Köln
2010

**Maria Sibylla Merian, Artist and Naturalist
1647 - 1717** Edited by Kurt Wettengl
Verlag Gerd Hatje

**Maria Sibylla Merian, Die Reise nach Surinam
1699** with text by Friedrich Schnack
(the second in Die Souvenir Reihe series)
Schuler Verlag, Stuttgart

Maria Sibylla Merian, Eine Biographie by
Helmut Kaiser
Piper Verlag, München 1999

Mediaeval Towns, The Story of Nuremberg by
Cecil Headlam
J. M. Dent and Sons 1911

New Book of Flowers by Maria Sibylla Merian
Prestel Verlag 1999 (reproduced by)

Die Sebalduskirche in Nürnberg by Hans-Martin
Barth Langewiesche - Bücherei 1988

**Seidenraupe, Dschungelblüte, Die
Lebensgeschichte der Maria Sibylla Merian**
by Charlotte Kerner Beltz & Gelberg 1989
**Siebenhundert Jahre Heilkunde in Frankfurt am
Main** by Wilhelm Kallmorgen
Verlag Moritz Diesterweg 1936

The Story of Nuremberg by Cecil Headlam
J. M. Dent & Sons, London 1911

ARCHIVES:

Landeskirchliches Archiv der Evangelisch-
Lutherischen Kirche in Bayern -- in Nürnberg
    Baptism record:
        Dorothea Helena Graff, February 2, 1678

LDS microfilm from the manuscripts in the city
archives, Frankfurt am Main
    Baptism records:
        Taufen 1642-1647 (bd.10) FHL INTL
FILM 341686
                Maria Sibylla Merian April 4, 1647

        Taufen 1648-1656 (bd.11) FHL INTL
FILM 341687
        Johann Maximillian Merian May 27, 1649
        Jacob Matthäus Marell June 15, 1654
        Maria Elisabeth Marell November 21, 1656

Marriage records:
Heiraten 1635-1657 (bd.4) FHL INTL FILM 341778
Johanna Merian and Jacob Marrel August 5, 1651

Heiraten 1658-1677 (bd.5) FHL INTL FILM 341779
Maria Sibylla Merian and Johann Graff May 16, 1665

Death records:
Tote 1636-1656 FHL INTL FILM 341810
Matthäus Merian May 1650
Johann Maximillian Merian November 30, 1651

Stadtarchiv and Museum of Bad Schwalbach
Information provided by Frau Dr. Bleymehl-Eiler

MISCELLANEOUS:

The church of Wiuwert (near the location of Castle Waltha)
Information about the Labadists
A copy of a map of Castle Waltha and its grounds by Johann Graff

German National Museum in Nürnberg
Albrecht Dürer's house/studio in Nürnberg
Fembohaus (city museum) in Nürnberg

http://www.altfrankfurt.com/   old Frankfurt history

old maps of Frankfurt, Nürnberg, Paramaribo

Stichting Surinaams Museum, Ft. Zeelandia, in
Paramaribo, Suriname
The Numismatic Museum in Paramaribo

72900806R00093

Made in the USA
Middletown, DE
09 May 2018